Storck shows us why this hasn't worked and, indeed, can't work. The section on usury is particularly important in understanding the ills which face our society.

—JOHN C. MÉDAILLE, author, *Toward a Truly Free Market: A Distributist Perspective*, *The Vocation of Business: Social Justice in the Marketplace*, *Theology: Mythos or Logos?*

In *Economics: An Alternative Introduction* Thomas Storck gives a powerful presentation of the shortcomings in how basic economics is taught and understood in the modern world, the most egregious of which is neglect of the very human element that is the reason economic activity exists. This book should be read by everyone who wants to claim they have any understanding of economics.

—DAVID W. COONEY, editor, *Practical Distributism*, author, *Distributism Basics: Foundational Principles*

ECONOMICS:
AN ALTERNATIVE INTRODUCTION

ECONOMICS

An Alternative Introduction

THOMAS STORCK

Foreword by Charles M. A. Clark

ISBN: 978-1-998492-17-6 (pbk)
ISBN: 978-1-998492-18-3 (hc)

XIII Books
An Imprint of Arouca Press
PO Box 55003
Bridgeport PO
Waterloo, ON N2J 0A5
Canada
www.aroucapress.com
Send inquiries to info@aroucapress.com

To the great Mother of God, Mary most holy.

CONTENTS

FOREWORD

CHARLES M. A. CLARK
Professor of Economics
St. John's University

At the start of the current millennium St. John Paul II called for a "new and deeper reflection on the nature of the economy and its purposes" (*World Day of Peace*, January 1, 2000). It has often been noted that economics is too important to be left solely to economists. With this book Thomas Storck has contributed to a deeper reflection on the nature and purpose of the economy by bringing Catholic social thought, especially the branch called "distributism," inspired by Leo XIII's call in *Rerum Novarum* for widely distributed property ownership, into a dialogue with Paul Samuelson's famous economics textbook. It is a clever way of comparing the principles of economics with the principles of Catholic social thought.

Interdisciplinary dialogue is a great challenge for economists, who used to refer to economics as the "queen of the social sciences." As a distinct discipline, economists make simplifying assumptions so that they can focus on "economic" motives, actions and outcomes, attempting to separate the "signal" from the "noise", or what they contend are the dominant and persistent factors from what is temporary and transient, and in doing so they lose contact with the other social sciences, and with its roots as a branch of moral philosophy. The historical and social richness of Adam Smith is replaced with equations. The problem is that nearly all motives, actions and outcomes in the economy are the result of more than just "economic" factors. Economic theory, especially the neoclassical economic theory taught to college freshmen, assumes individuals pursue their narrow self-interest, influenced only by their preferences (which are autonomous), prices and their budget. This is the "rational economic man" model adopted by neoclassical economic theory, also known as "*homo economicus*". This, and other simplifying assumptions, are justified by economists because they facilitate the use of mathematics in economics, making economic theory more like the hard sciences (although we should note that many economists are true believers of the "rational economic man" model as an accurate portrayal of human nature). Yet, as Robert Heilbroner famously quipped, "The prestige accorded to mathematics in economics has given it rigor, but, alas, also mortis."[1] Mortis here is due to a loss of historical and social context, which includes the roles that culture and power play in shaping economic motives, actions and outcomes. What is assumed away is often the very glue that holds society together.

A deeper and more complete understanding of the economy and its place in the lives of individuals and communities would include other disciplines that provide insights into the human experience. This starts with the most fundamental question underlying all social analysis: what does it mean to be human? Let us look at just one basic aspect of being human—consuming food. Humans are physical animals that need to eat to stay alive. Here we might start our investigation with some input from a nutritionist. Next, we might examine issues on the growth of food (a horticulturalist) as well as the army of experts on the preparation of food, prevention of the contamination of food and the safe storage and transportation of food, so it can be eventually eaten by humans. Economists enter this story when a community uses prices to allocate which tasks people perform and what resources go into food production

---

[1] Heilbroner, Robert L. 1979. "Modern Economics as a Chapter in the History of Economic Thought," *History of Political Economy*, Vol. 11, No. 2, pp. 192–198.

and other human activities (exchanges between food production and other sectors of the economy). Of course, many other disciplines are involved in this process, yet all this technical expertise does not capture the role food plays in strengthening communal bonds and in the lived experience of actual humans and in the meaning they attach to their "daily bread," a meaning that certainly shapes all the activities mentioned above. Attendance at nearly any extended family holiday dinner will easily prove my point. The social investigator needs to go deeper, ending up in the disciplines of philosophy and theology. Here is where Thomas Storck's contribution to understanding the economy starts, for he asserts that the economic life of humans is "of humans." The relationship between philosophy and economics has been well understood, at least by historians of economic thought, and by the leading economists, most of whom studied philosophy before making their contributions to economic theory. Adam Smith, often called the founder of modern economics, was a Professor of Moral Philosophy, and economics was taught as part of moral philosophy into the 20th century in some universities. The contribution from theology to understanding economic actions and outcomes has been less studied and is admittedly controversial. Yet the dialogue between Catholic social thought and economics does not include the claim that the discipline of theology should replace economics. Christianity is not like Judaism or Islam in that it does not have a political or economic order laid out in its sacred texts. All of the modern popes (post Leo XIII) have made it clear that the Church's social teaching is not a substitute for economics and the other social sciences. Yet, economic theory becomes excessively narrow when it is closed off from the insights of other disciplines.

In the mid-19th century St. John Henry Newman dealt with this very issue in his famous lectures published as *The Idea of a University*, where he pointed out the problems that arise when economic theory was cut off from the humanities (including theology) and other social sciences:

> I only say that, though they [economists] speak truth, they do not speak the whole truth; that they speak a narrow truth, and think it a broad truth; that their deductions must be compared with other truths, which are acknowledged to be truths, in order to verify, complete, and correct them. They say what is true, *exceptis excipiendis*; . . . true, but not the measure of all things; true, but if thus inordinately, extravagantly, ruinously carried out, in spite of other sciences, in spite of Theology, sure to become but a great bubble, and to burst.

One can look at Newman's observation as prophetic, given that one of the central conclusions of economic orthodoxy during Newman's time, as well as our own, is that markets are inherently efficient and self-correcting (Efficient Market Hypothesis today, Say's Law of Markets in the 19th century) yet a long series of financial crisis from Newman's time to our own shows that this is not always the case. Pope Francis (*Evangelii Gaudium*, no. 55) linked the 2009 financial crisis with the excessively narrow view of human nature that underlies how the economy is understood, when he wrote:

> The current financial crisis can make us overlook the fact that it originated in a profound human crisis: the denial of the primacy of the human person! We have created new idols. The worship of the ancient golden calf (cf. *Ex* 32:1–35) has returned in a new and ruthless guise in the idolatry of money and the dictatorship of an impersonal economy lacking a truly human purpose. The worldwide crisis affecting finance and the economy lays bare their imbalances and, above all, their lack of real concern for human beings; man is reduced to one of his needs alone: consumption.

While Catholic social teaching is not a competing economic theory or economic model, it does assert that a broader view of the human person would greatly improve our understanding of the economy.

With this book Thomas Storck brings Catholic social thought into dialogue with mainstream economics. The role of dialogue in Catholic social thought needs to be emphasized, for Catholic social thought is necessarily dialogical. It always starts with reading the "signs of the times," or as Leo XIII noted "Nothing is more useful than to look upon the world as it really is" (*Rerum Novarum*, no. 18). Catholic social thought needs to be in dialogue with contemporary reality to be relevant and understands that reality requires engaging the various disciplines which modern society uses to understand and explain their reality. Thus, when Catholic social thought engages issues of medical ethics, it is in dialogue with medical professionals and ethicists. In the case of this book, Thomas Storck's primary dialogue partner is Paul Samuelson, the Dean of American mainstream economics.

Samuelson's influence on the economics profession would be hard to exaggerate. While he is not at the level of the "worldly philosophers" (Adam Smith, David Ricardo, Karl Marx, and John Maynard Keynes), Samuelson did shape the dominant paradigm of post-World War II economic theory more than any other economist. Samuelson's lasting influence came from an idea and a book, neither of which were mentioned in his 1970 Nobel Prize in Economics citation. The idea is the "grand neoclassical synthesis" which was the reconciliation of Keynesian macroeconomics with neoclassical (marginal utility theory) microeconomics (John Hicks first combined the two, but eventually recognized that they did not fit easily together). And the book was his *Economics: An Introductory Analysis*, the most successful economics textbook of all time (since 2001 co-written with William Nordhaus). My first exposure to economics (late 1970s) was with the 10th edition of Samuelson's book. Nearly every textbook I have looked at in my 40 years of teaching economics is based on Samuelson.

Samuelson's textbook presented neoclassical microeconomics, which focuses on individual economic behavior and how individual markets functioned (what used to be called price theory) in one semester and Keynesian macroeconomics, which examines aggregate economic concepts such as economic growth, unemployment and inflation, in a second semester. Generally, most students did not figure out that the basic premise of the first semester (that markets always worked towards equilibrium) was violated in the second semester where it was clear that aggregate markets (like the labor market) did not always, or often, produce a market clearing equilibrium (full employment in this case). To achieve the neoclassical synthesis Samuelson had to reduce what was revolutionary in John Maynard Keynes' contributions to economics (the role of uncertainty and historical time in economic decision-making). Keynes' great insight on uncertainty relates ultimately to a different understanding of the human person, which I would argue is the root cause of most fundamental disagreements in economics. Thomas Storck's contrasting Catholic social thought and its ideas and principles with those which we find in Samuelson's textbook is a welcome addition to the rethinking of economics. John Maynard Keynes noted that he had a "long struggle to escape" the ideas that shaped how the economy was then understood, and he noted that such an escape required a reexamining of the basic premises of the current orthodoxy. The need to rethink the current orthodoxy in economics was made obvious during the Financial Meltdown of 2008 (which caught nearly all leading economists by surprise) and the inability of economics as a disciple to learn and adjust to the reality of financial instability. It is also being demonstrated by the reality of climate change as a life-threatening externality, linked to pursuing economic growth at all costs (what has become known as the need to go beyond GDP). But most importantly for Thomas Storck, it is the reality that decades of pursuing economic growth, either by countries or as the main purpose of individual humans, is not making people happier or promoting human flourishing. The central question is not: what is the right monetary policy? or should we raise or lower taxes? or how do we have full employment and price stability? (Samuelson's goal for economics). These are often important questions, but they can only be meaningfully engaged after we have examined the nature and purpose of the economy.

We are again at a point in the history of economic thought where perspectives from outside of the economic profession are entering and influencing economic discourse. We see this most clearly in the role that psychology has played in the rise of behavioral economics (a very popular but so far not very fruitful branch of economics). Most of the past progress in the history of economic thought has come from outside influences (Adam Smith and Newtonian mechanics being one such example). It is only by engaging in dialogue with other disciplines and other approaches to economics that economic orthodoxy has ever improved and become more useful. This book is a contribution to this necessary dialogue.

PREFACE

This book is intended as a popular introduction to economics. It has been written as a counterpoise to mainstream neoclassical economics, the kind of economics that is taught most frequently today and that the casual student of economics is likely to encounter. The reader will see that I am in constant dialog, or better, contestation, with the late Paul Samuelson, probably the best known exponent of that kind of economics, and his clear presentation of its principles serves as an excellent foil. Moreover, I have written this book with reference to the social doctrine of the Catholic Church, which, "the Church offers . . . as an *indispensable and ideal orientation*" (*Centesimus Annus*, no. 43). Not that I am writing a book only for Catholics or whose argument depends upon any kind of religious commitment. But simply that as a Catholic I see no need to separate my thinking about economics from my Catholic faith, and so I have not hesitated not only to cite the Church's social doctrine, but to include appeals to Holy Scripture and to our last end, eternal life with God. For natural and revealed knowledge, though largely distinct, are not opposed, and in fact, any genuine concept of a science such as economics, will recognize its dependence upon higher sciences, including moral theology. Therefore I assume the position taken by Pius XI in *Quadragesimo Anno* (no. 42), that

> though economic activity and moral discipline are guided each by its own principles in its own sphere, it is false that the two orders are so distinct and alien that the former in no way depends on the latter. The laws of economics, as they are called, derived from the nature of earthly goods and from the qualities of the human body and soul, determine what aims

> are unattainable or attainable in economic matters
> and what means are thereby necessary. But reason
> itself clearly deduces from the nature of things and
> from the individual and social character of man,
> what is the end and object of the whole economic
> order assigned by God the Creator.

Still the book is intended not as an introduction to
Catholic social teaching, but as an introduction to
economics proper.

It will be obvious to any reader that I deal with economics at a very basic level. I do this because I am
writing for those who have studied economics only at
the elementary level, or who have perhaps not studied
it formally at all, but have picked up some notions of
it here and there from commentators and editorial
writers, notions which most likely are based ultimately
on the neoclassical model. But this model, I contend,
offers largely a mistaken approach to its subject and
creates a false image of economic activity. Hence, as
I see it, there is a great need to undo many popular
notions of how economies work, about the nature and
role of economic laws, and so on. My purpose then is
limited: To provide what I think is a more accurate
foundation for understanding economics, both as a
subject and an activity, and to correct the widespread
misunderstandings that seem to be endemic to the
popular mind, especially it seems in the United States.
I regard this book as, in a certain way, akin to Henry
Hazlitt's *Economics in One Lesson*. Although I disagree
profoundly with Hazlitt's approach to and understanding of economics, he aimed at a popular readership with
a non-technical presentation of how, in his opinion,
economies functioned.

Much of this text is based on articles, online and
print, which I have written over several decades, especially in *The Distributist Review* and *Practical Distributism*.
It was suggested to me that I should collect these

articles into a book, but it seemed to me better to try to create a more or less connected and orderly discussion of the different aspects and parts of economics. So I have freely altered and combined these articles, added new material, and tried to eliminate or at least reduce repetitions, although some necessarily remain.

Although I am a distributist, I have not intended to write an introduction to or justification of distributism. At times it will be necessary to contrast distributism with capitalism, simply because we live in a capitalist economy and much of our economic activity and thinking is understandable only in that context. So frequently I need to show how and why the capitalist approach is not the only possible approach. And so although most of the articles upon which this book is based were originally written on behalf of distributism and many of the references to distributism remain, I have omitted many of them in order to make this book, as much as possible, an introduction simply to economics.

I wish to thank Professor Charles Clark for his kindness in writing a foreword to this volume, and my wife Inez Storck, who is always generous in taking time from her own work as a translator to review my work and make useful suggestions for improvement.

Thomas Storck
September 2024

SECTION I

Foundations

1
What Starting Point for Economics?

How we begin a discussion of something often goes a long way to determine the conclusion we arrive at. For example, if we begin a discussion of human sexuality simply by noting the nearly ubiquitous desire for sexual pleasure, that might well put our discussion on the wrong track, and we might decide that the purpose of our efforts was to figure out how to extend and increase everyone's opportunity for sexual pleasure at any time or place, and with any person. On the other hand, if we were to begin by noting the fact that human sexuality is related to a very important social function, that of the continuation of the human race, we might reach very different conclusions. The same is true of a discussion of economics.

As a social, or perhaps better, a *human* science, economics necessarily seeks its starting point in the conduct or actions of human beings. But, as suggested above, there are many different and conflicting starting points from which to look at the activities of mankind. The single aspect of our behavior, however, that is generally taken as the starting point for economic analysis today, according to most authors and teachers, involves *scarcity*. This starting point necessarily tends to direct the discussion in a particular direction. Here is how Paul Samuelson introduces the topic.

> A situation of scarcity is one in which goods are limited relative to desires. An objective observer would have to agree that, even after two centuries of rapid economic growth, production in the United

States is simply not high enough to meet everyone's desires. If you add up all the wants, you quickly find that there are simply not enough goods and services to satisfy even a small fraction of everyone's consumption desires. Our national output would have to be many times larger before the average American could live at the level of the average doctor or big-league baseball player.[1]

I suggest that here we have something like the original sin of mainstream economics. In a way, of course, Samuelson's statement is true: "Our national output would have to be many times larger before the average American could live at the level of the average doctor or big-league baseball player." But is this the right starting point for the study of economics? Is it the most important thing we can say about our activities of production and exchange? In fact, Samuelson's statement leads us astray and vitiates his entire concept of what economics, both as an activity and as a subject of study, is about.

Let us begin by examining Samuelson's assertion carefully. "A situation of scarcity is one in which goods are limited relative to desires." In the first place we can note a curious fact, namely that the author makes no distinction between our wants and our needs. Although some thinkers would deny that there is any objective difference between these, common sense and ordinary usage recognize such a difference. Few would deny that having enough to eat and desiring to take a luxury vacation are fundamentally different things. But for Samuelson, apparently a desire to "live at the level of the average doctor or big-league baseball player" is no different from a desire to have enough to eat or to provide medical care for a sick child. But can any Christian, or any rational person, really think that God gave mankind the capacity and need to use external goods so

---

[1] Paul A. Samuelson and William D. Nordhaus, *Microeconomics* (Boston: McGraw-Hill Irwin, 17th ed., 2001), p. 4.

that we all "could live at the level of the average doctor or big-league baseball player"? Surely we can say that Samuelson's utter failure even to attempt to distinguish between needs and wants marks his brand of economic analysis as faulty from the start. For however much we might quibble about where to draw the line between a want and a need, everyone really recognizes that they are different.

And secondly, Samuelson does not attempt to prove, he simply assumes not only that everyone desires to "live at the level of the average doctor or big-league baseball player," but that this is what economists and economic policy makers should concern themselves with. But is this true, is it really the case that most people want to "live at the level of the average doctor or big-league baseball player"? Here we come to the interesting question of the effects of culture on our desires. It may be the case that most Americans wish to live at that level, but why is that? Over fifty years ago Msgr. John Tracy Ellis, in his once-famous address, *American Catholics and the Intellectual Life*, wrote,

> From the time when the Duc de Liancourt traveled through the states along the eastern seaboard in the 1790's and wrote one of the earliest books by a foreigner on the new Republic, to the essays of recent observers like Evelyn Waugh, few visitors from abroad have neglected to comment on the American attachment to material goods and the desire to make a fortune as dominant characteristics of our society.[2]

---

[2] John Tracy Ellis, *American Catholics and the Intellectual Life* (Chicago: Heritage Foundation, 1956), p. 27. Statements like these could be multiplied almost without end. The famous French observer of American life, Alexis de Tocqueville, wrote of Americans that "one usually finds that love of money is either the chief or a secondary motive at the bottom of everything the Americans do," and "The American will describe as noble and estimable ambition that which our medieval ancestors would have called base cupidity." *Democracy in America*, vol. II, part III, chaps. 17 and 18.

But are such desires dominant always and everywhere? There is considerable evidence that they are not. If we consider simply modern examples from the Western world, we have the interesting testimony of Max Weber about nineteenth century cloth merchants.

> Until about the middle of the past [i.e., nineteenth] century, the life of a putter-out was, at least in many of the branches of the Continental textile industry, what we should to-day consider very comfortable.... The number of business hours was very moderate, perhaps five to six a day, sometimes considerably less; in the rush season, where there was one, more. Earnings were moderate; enough to lead a respectable life and in good times to put away a little. On the whole, relations among competitors were relatively good, with a large degree of agreement on the fundamentals of business. A long daily visit to the tavern, with often plenty to drink, and a congenial circle of friends, made life comfortable and leisurely.[3]

As well we have the testimony of former Dutch Prime Minister Ruud Lubbers

> that the Dutch are not aiming to maximize gross national product per capita [but] are seeking to attain a high quality of life, a just, participatory and sustainable society [in which] the number of working hours per citizen are rather limited [and] there is more room for all those important aspects of our lives that are not part of our jobs, for which we are not paid and for which there is never enough time.[4]

If it is true that most Americans might want to "live at the level of the average doctor or big-league baseball

---

[3] Max Weber, *The Protestant Ethic and the Spirit of Capitalism* (New York: Charles Scribner's, [1904–5] 1958, pp. 66–67.
[4] Quoted in Anders Hayden, "Europe's Work-Time Alternatives" in John de Graaf, ed., *Take Back Your Time: Fighting Overwork and Time Poverty in America*, (San Francisco: Berrett-Koehler, 2003), p. 202.

player," the reasons are no doubt complex, but they definitely include the fact that our entire culture is permeated by the notion that acquisition of material goods and pleasures is the *summum bonum* of man's life. This idea is reinforced not just by advertising, but by most of the media which concentrates on new gadgets, fancy clothes, expensive vacations and the like, and even by our understanding of the purpose of education, which is usually seen exclusively in terms of a return on investment. It would seem that Samuelson has simply taken a characteristic of his own culture and assumed it as a constant of human nature.

No doubt nearly everyone can be taught to desire more and more, can have his tastes corrupted or inflamed by materialistic advertising, just as nearly everyone can be taught not to be content with one spouse but to actively seek sexual satisfaction with as many partners as possible. For like our material wants, our sexual wants can also be looked upon as "unlimited," and people can be taught in both cases to see these desires as fundamental and legitimate needs. But it is in great part our cultural mores that teach us that we have "unlimited wants" for stuff and that these wants are so important as to justify the whole apparatus of modern economies and modern economics, as likewise it is in part cultural mores that can make us dissatisfied with one spouse. It is true that in both instances such desires are rooted in our fallen human nature, but we have the choice either to inflame such desires, e.g., via advertising or pornography, or to use cultural and other means to promote contentment and satisfaction instead.

Let us consider another criticism of using scarcity as the starting point of economics. God has given mankind both the need for external goods and the capacity to produce or acquire them. Except in circumstances of drought or other natural disaster, one man generally has the ability to produce food or other goods which more than satisfy his own physical needs. If that were not the case, then no one in any civilization would ever have been able to devote his time to works of religion or learning or war or government. But farmers and craftsmen were usually able to provide for themselves with something left over. What can we learn from this? We might learn that a possible starting point for economic analysis is the fact that God has given to the human race an ability to provide for its material needs and even something beyond our basic needs so that we have been able to create high civilizations, works of art, and so on. Instead of scarcity, could we not regard mankind's God-given economic sufficiency as the most basic economic fact? And if we do, then what implications might we draw from that? Instead of seeing human existence as a struggle between man and nature or between individuals to fulfill our limitless consumption desires, we might begin to thank and glorify God who has given such bounty to this world, even in its fallen state.

But let us begin over again with the question that was implied at the outset of this discussion, the question of purpose, which in any human or natural activity is the overriding and fundamental matter to be considered. When we look at the economic conduct of mankind and ask ourselves why the human race engages in such activities, I suppose that everyone would admit that we do so in order to produce goods and services for our use. But for what end? St. Thomas Aquinas wrote that "... the appetite of natural riches is not infinite, because according to a set measure they satisfy nature; but the appetite of artificial riches is infinite, because it serves inordinate concupiscence...."[5] St. Thomas was here contrasting real economic goods — "natural

---

[5] *Summa Theologiae*, I-II, q. 2, a. 1 ad 3.

riches" — with "artificial riches" — money and other surrogates for real wealth. The former aim to "satisfy nature," and there is generally a limit on how much of them we desire to possess, for there is only so much *stuff* which any person can actually use, and if we acquire more than that, we must resort to devices such as renting storage bins in order to keep our extra and unnecessary possessions, something which in St. Thomas' time happily did not exist. But whatever serves "inordinate concupiscence," serves to satisfy not our reasonable needs but whatever desires we might have, such as the desire to "live at the level of the average doctor or big-league baseball player."

I should note that Aquinas is not asserting that it is only our basic needs for food or shelter or clothing that are natural. The purposes for which we need material goods can be broadly divided into two parts: first, the absolutely necessary goods, sufficient food, water, shelter, to keep the human race alive. But if we stopped there we would be like ants or bees. They also engage in work to provide for themselves these necessities of life. Human beings, however, are rational animals, that is, our capacities surpass the merely material level, and hence for us a proper human life is not limited simply to survival. We need objects of beauty, music, books, even devices and inventions that make life easier or save time and effort. Without these a properly human life is impossible or difficult. But all the same, St. Thomas sets up human nature and its needs as the standard against which man's economic activity must be measured, in contrast to Samuelson who simply takes each and every demand for a good or service as a given, however much "it serves inordinate concupiscence."

Closely connected with the idea of scarcity is that of economic efficiency. We may introduce this subject by way of Adam Smith's discussion in the very first chapter of *The Wealth of Nations* about the division of labor in the production of pins. He contrasts the probable output of "a workman not educated to this business ... nor acquainted with the use of the machinery employed in it" with the output of a process of specialization in which "[o]ne man draws out the wire, another straights it, a third cuts it, a fourth points it, a fifth grinds it at the top for receiving the head," so that "the important business of making a pin is ... divided into about eighteen distinct operations." In the first case, that of the "workman not educated to this business," Smith avers that he "could scarce ... make one pin in a day, and certainly could not make twenty," while on the other hand, ten men working according to even an imperfect division of labor "could make among them upwards of forty-eight thousand pins ... in a day."

Securing an adequate supply of pins, however, was not what Smith was really concerned about here, but as he himself says, with the principle of the division of labor, and with the resulting increase in output, of which the production of pins was only one example. "The division of labour, however, so far as it can be introduced, occasions, in every art, a proportionable increase of the productive powers of labour." In general this is true, of course, and such division has been a means of multiplying the productive capacities of human work. If we increase the "productive powers of labour" so that the resulting output is greater, we are said to increase *economic efficiency*, to get a larger output from the same input, as when we go from ten lone workmen who might altogether produce fewer than a hundred pins a day to ten working according to a division of labor who could make "upwards of forty-eight thousand pins" in the same time.

The benefits of economic efficiency might seem obvious and in a way they are. But in current economics efficiency is closely connected to the claim we examined above, that of limited resources and unlimited desires. "Given unlimited wants, it is important that an economy make the best use of its limited resources. That brings us to the critical notion of efficiency."[6] The division of labor, then, and more broadly, everything that contributes to economic efficiency as a means for increasing production, is premised upon the notion of a necessarily finite amount of resources and goods and mankind's unlimited wants.

I am not, certainly, suggesting that we should seek economic *in*efficiency. Rather, it is that by equating economic efficiency with an imperative to produce as much stuff as possible, we assume both that the human race has "unlimited wants," and that fulfilling these is an economic, if not an ethical, imperative. Thus anything that gets in the way of economic efficiency or economic growth becomes suspect. Environmental regulations, for example, are often criticized for their adverse effect, real or imagined, on economic activity or industrial productivity. Of course, sometimes an environmental regulation can be stupid or ill-conceived or produce little real benefit. But the charge that a certain regulation inhibits economic activity or even job creation is meaningless unless the regulation in question can be shown to be frivolous or of limited value. For it is surely absurd to think that the only thing that matters is whether or not we have increased production and that we do not need clean water or clear air, as long as we can go on producing more gadgets of some kind or other. It is not much of a benefit to produce goods or even provide jobs in exchange for living in unhealthy surroundings. If the only way that our society can provide jobs for its citizens or provide us with the necessities of life is via processes that harm the environment in which we must all live, this surely argues that something is fundamentally wrong with our industrial economy.

---

[6] Samuelson, *Microeconomics*, p. 4.

That is what needs to be addressed, instead of seeking a cheap way out by offering society the choice of two evils, unemployment or filthy air and water.

Mankind surely needs external goods. But these are needed not as ends in themselves nor, since man's needs are finite, can our need for goods be infinite. If by economic efficiency we mean not wasting our resources or our time and effort, well and good. But if economic efficiency is understood as an imperative to produce as much as possible to fulfill our alleged "unlimited wants," then there is every reason to question it. And even if man truly has "unlimited wants," as Samuelson believes, those wants are not necessarily worthy of respect, any more than someone's desire for multiple sexual partners is. But by making the concept of economic efficiency one of the foundations of economics, economists are telling us that the attempt to fulfill the allegedly "unlimited wants" of the human race — even if these are for mere baubles — is at the apex of social goods. Just as we would rightly reject a sociology that made our desire for unlimited sexual pleasure its foundation, so we ought to reject an economics that makes our desire, whether real or imagined, for unlimited goods its foundation.

I do not think that I need to belabor which of the two attitudes toward economic activity and material things that I have sketched here ought to characterize a Christian of any type. Holy Scripture itself is quite clear on this point:

> . . . if we have food and clothing, with these we shall be content. But those who desire to be rich fall into temptation, into a snare, into many senseless and hurtful desires that plunge men into ruin and destruction. For the love of money is the root of all evils; it is through this craving that some have wandered away from the faith and pierced their hearts with many pangs. (1 Tim. 6:8–10)

In *Centesimus Annus* St. John Paul II speaks of "the right to possess the things necessary for one's personal development and the development of one's family" (no. 6). And in the same encyclical he writes in another passage (no. 36),

> It is not wrong to want to live better; what is wrong is a style of life which is presumed to be better when it is directed toward "having" rather than "being," which wants to have more, not in order to be more but in order to spend life in enjoyment as an end in itself.

Now I realize that it is not always easy to say how much is "necessary for one's personal development and the development of one's family." In fact, there is apt to be disagreement about what is a reasonable standard that satisfies nature. And to some extent such disagreement is to be expected, for it is impossible to calculate such a standard with mathematical exactness. But the important thing, and certainly the first thing to do, is to recognize that mankind's economic activity and the products that result therefrom do have a purpose, namely, to "satisfy nature," and not to satisfy simply any and every desire prompted by the wish to live in the manner of a major-league baseball player. At some point, any sensible person will have to admit that the needs of nature have been satisfied, and that anything beyond that is simply excess.

Now, what logically follows from this? We can apply the teaching of St. Paul, St. Thomas, and St. John Paul not only to individuals and families, but also to societies. Although many individuals and families do seek in some degree to acquire and use material goods according to the stipulations and warnings just cited, in a society such as ours this is not easy to do, and, as I said, it is often very difficult to decide what is a reasonable standard of living that will satisfy nature, especially since American society can make it difficult to live a countercultural life. In this regard I will note only two things.

First, as Benedict XVI wrote in his encyclical *Caritas in Veritate* (no. 37), "every economic decision has a moral consequence." Since the kinds of stores we patronize, the kinds of products we buy and use, have effects that are economic, environmental and also cultural, therefore they have both moral and spiritual consequences for each of us. A person who desires to "live at the level of the average doctor or big-league baseball player" is making decisions which not only have moral consequences that affect others but unavoidably shape that person's soul according to a particular pattern. A lifetime of our economic decisions will determine whether we have shaped ourselves according to the image of Samuelson's economic man or to the opposite pattern suggested by Holy Scripture and the writings of the saints.

Secondly, just as it is very difficult for someone raised in a society saturated by pornography and sexual promiscuity to realize what a sane and healthy sexuality is, so it is hard for those who were raised in a commercial society, a society which more or less makes riches and material goods an idol, to realize what a sane attitude toward work and material goods is. In both cases we have to strive, using all the means of grace available, to form sound judgments. But now I want to turn our attention to the question of society as a whole, that is, about how a society that seeks to orient its productive activity primarily toward satisfying nature might conduct itself.

The following is a description, from Richard Tawney's seminal book, *Religion and the Rise of Capitalism*, of the outlook of Medieval Europe toward work and material goods.

> Material riches are necessary; they have a secondary importance, since without them men cannot support themselves and help one another; the wise

ruler, as St. Thomas said, will consider in founding his State the natural resources of the country. But economic motives are suspect. Because they are powerful appetites, men fear them, but they are not mean enough to applaud them. Like other strong passions, what they need, it is thought, is not a clear field, but repression. There is no place in medieval theory for economic activity which is not related to a moral end, and to found a science of society upon the assumption that the appetite for economic gain is a constant and measurable force, to be accepted, like other natural forces, as an inevitable and self-evident *datum* would have appeared to the medieval thinker as hardly less irrational or less immoral than to make the premise of social philosophy the unrestrained operation of such necessary human attributes as pugnacity or the sexual instinct.

And he continues with his description of medieval economic ethics:

At every turn, therefore, there are limits, restrictions, warnings, against allowing economic interests to interfere with serious affairs. It is right for a man to seek such wealth as is necessary for a livelihood in his station. To seek more is not enterprise, but avarice, and avarice is a deadly sin. Trade is legitimate; the different resources of different countries show that it was intended by Providence. But it is a dangerous business. A man must be sure that he carries it on for the public benefit, and that the profits which he takes are no more than the wages of his labor.[7]

And another historian wrote along similar lines,

We can, therefore, lay down as the first principle of mediaeval economics that there was a limit to money-making imposed by the purpose for which the money was made. Each worker had to keep in

---

[7] Richard H. Tawney, *Religion and the Rise of Capitalism*, (New York: Harcourt, Brace, 1926), pp. 31–32.

front of himself the aim of his life and consider the acquiring of money as a means only to an end, which at one and the same time justified and limited him. When, therefore, sufficiency had been obtained there could be no reason for continuing further efforts at getting rich, . . . except in order to help others.[8]

The question to consider now concerns how a truly Christian society would implement these ideals. Many people, certainly most Americans, would think that adherence to such standards must be something purely voluntary. At most, the Church would seek to persuade people of its desirability via her preaching and catechesis. And certainly that is the first thing to be done, to create a social consciousness that the pursuit of riches beyond what one needs is both criminal and stupid. Criminal because it helps create a society that upholds false ideals and corrupts our souls, stupid because it detracts from what life in this world is about, and above all, because it makes more difficult our attainment of eternal life. I am not asserting that it is a sin simply to be rich, but I do assert that riches are almost always a near occasion of sin, and therefore, if we are rich, we had better be careful about the effect on our souls. And especially do we need a good justification for seeking more riches if we already have enough so that the demands of nature are satisfied.

But there is more. If we notice what Tawney said in the passage I just quoted, "At every turn, therefore, there are limits, restrictions, warnings, against allowing economic interests to interfere with serious affairs," a Christian society will not be content to simply use moral persuasion in order to correctly orient our attitude toward work and material goods. If nothing else, such a society will make it rather hard for someone to get rich. It will certainly do nothing to facilitate such

---

[8] Bede Jarrett, *Social Theories of the Middle Ages*, (Westminster, Md.: Newman, 1942), pp. 157–158.

acquisition of riches, and it will try to structure its laws, tax code and general economic arrangements so that it is easy to earn enough to support one's family, but hard to do much more.

Many are familiar with the taxation scheme suggested by Hilaire Belloc in his 1936 book, *The Restoration of Property*,[9] according to which any enterprise which exceeded a certain size would be taxed at such a high rate that no one would expand his business or landholdings beyond a modest size. I know that many people have an instinctive violent reaction against such proposals, but those who do should ask themselves a couple questions. How is this an unjust restriction? How is anyone's true good harmed by such laws? Until recently we as a society in the United States saw this clearly with regard to that other great human appetite, sexual satisfaction. Within the lifetime of many of us divorce was in most states difficult to obtain, pornography was strictly regulated or even prohibited, homosexual activity illegal. And laws on the books in some states forbade adultery, even if they were rarely enforced. Even today prostitution is illegal in nearly every state. We justified these restrictions by saying that such activity was contrary to both the natural law and the revealed law of God, harmful to individuals and to the social order, and that therefore the free choices and desires of individuals could justly be limited in such matters.

If we are serious about conforming our lives to the norms of morality with regard to money and property, the same argument applies: "those who desire to be rich fall into temptation, into a snare, into many senseless and hurtful desires that plunge men into ruin and destruction." The disordered striving after riches is as hurtful to the common good as is the disordered striving after sexual pleasure. Both material wealth and sexual pleasure are true goods, but they are goods

---

[9] Currently available from IHS Press.

only in their rightful places. No one's genuine freedom or legitimate rights are infringed upon if the pursuit of wealth is hindered and directed toward legitimate channels, even by use of state power, just as no one's genuine freedom or legitimate rights are infringed upon by legal restrictions on disordered sexual behavior.

There is a wonderful quote from G. K. Chesterton in *What's Wrong With the World* that juxtaposes so well these two areas of human behavior.

> I am well aware that the word "property" has been defiled in our time by the corruption of the great capitalists. One would think, to hear people talk that the Rothchilds and the Rockefellers were on the side of property. But obviously they are the enemies of property; because they are enemies of their own limitations. They do not want their own land; but other people's.... It is the negation of property that the Duke of Sutherland should have all the farms in one estate; just as it would be the negation of marriage if he had all our wives in one harem.[10]

If it is proper to prevent the Duke of Sutherland from obtaining all of our women as his wives, why is it not proper to prevent him from obtaining all the property as his own?

If, therefore, a society attempts to channel its economic activity toward the common good, it in no way infringes on legitimate human freedom in the economic realm. Rather it provides the necessary means by which economic activity can attain its true end: not the goods and services that satisfy everyone's consumption desires, but those that satisfy the appetite for natural riches which according to a set measure satisfy nature. This is true wisdom, both human and Christian, this is the teaching of the Church, the command of Holy Scripture, and the sure way toward our eternal salvation.

---

[10] Part I, chapter 6.

2

Economics and
the Real World

An article some years ago in *The Economist* about economic bubbles noted, "Many economists have struggled to accept that bubbles exist, as that is difficult to square with the idea of efficient markets."[1] That is to say, economists struggle to accept the evidence before their eyes since that is difficult to square with their *a priori* theoretical construct. Although economists are not the only practitioners of an academic discipline who prefer their models and theories to reality, they are perhaps the worst offenders in that respect. Economists have erected an edifice of enormous sophistication and complexity, which, sad to say, often bears little resemblance to the real world. The chief structural component of this edifice is the market, the quasi-magical process by which all that is out of kilter in the world can be made right.

"[B]ubbles [are] difficult to square with the idea of efficient markets." How do we explain such a flight toward unreality? It is because of the fundamental postulate that allegedly explains all economic conduct that such a disconnect can exist.

> Two centuries ago, Adam Smith proclaimed that, through the workings of the invisible hand, those who pursue their own self-interest in a competitive economy will most effectively promote the public interest. This concept — that the rough-and-tumble of market competition is a potent force for raising

---

[1] "Not fully Inflated," December 7, 2013.

output and living standards—is one of the most
profound and powerful ideas in history. . . . [2]

As I said in the preceding chapter, generally contemporary economists base their work primarily on the
twin principles of scarcity and efficiency, and upon the
underlying conception of human nature and human
behavior as simply a constant struggle to fulfill our
desires. On these two pillars, and based on their simplistic refusal to distinguish between needs and wants,
they have erected a sophisticated superstructure which
produces a remarkably coherent account of our economic behavior and outcomes—on paper at least. But
as we just saw, "economists have struggled to accept
that bubbles exist, as that is difficult to square with
the idea of efficient markets." But if reality gets in the
way of one of the foundational ideas of one's science,
then perhaps it is that foundational idea, not reality
that should be changed? And so before proceeding
in the following chapters with a discussion of various
aspects of our economic life, such as money, prices,
wages and so on, in this chapter I continue my critique
of mainstream economic doctrine by noting some of
the specific points where the intricate superstructure
that economists have erected over their twin ideas of
scarcity and efficiency suffers from a major disconnect
with the real world and with the actual operations of
economies. And I propose to do so using again the
statements of Samuelson and his associates, letting
them be witnesses against themselves, as it were.

In the first place, to grasp the conception of economics that Samuelson and the vast majority of professional economists champion, we must recognize
that they want to make economic behavior as much
like the behavior of physical objects as possible. Just as
you can drop a stone of a certain weight from a certain

---

[2] Samuelson, *Microeconomics*, p. 286.

height and measure how fast it falls, how big an impact it makes on what it hits, etc., and create graphs and equations based on this, so these economists want to make the economic behavior of human beings as much like stones as possible. Are these economists successful in this? Let us look at some examples.

The fundamental principle of market behavior, according to mainstream economists, is to maximize our economic satisfaction or what is known as utility, in fact, to buy cheap and to sell dear, as Adam Smith expressed it. Now while I certainly do not deny that in general there is such a tendency on the part of humanity, it does not follow either that this is always the strongest influence on human behavior or that other forces, e.g., economic power or cultural and legal norms, do not significantly modify how this tendency works out in actual life.

In explaining market behavior Samuelson gives pride of place to an explanation of what are known as perfectly competitive markets. He defines this type of market in these words.

> Perfect competition is the world of *price-takers*. A perfectly competitive firm sells a homogeneous product (one identical to the product sold by others in the industry). It is so small relative to its market that it cannot affect the market price; it simply takes the price as given.[3]

A common example of this type of producer (firm) is a small farmer who grows a crop, say tomatoes, essentially identical with the crop of other tomato farmers. Each individual small tomato farmer must simply accept the going price. There is nothing he can do to change that price as long as his output remains small and his product undifferentiated from that of other tomato-growers. The problem with this arises because Samuelson and

---

[3] *Microeconomics*, p. 148.

his school consider this type of competition as the norm, whereas even according to neoclassical economic analysis perfect competition is rare. After describing such markets, in the next chapter Samuelson writes: "Perfectly competitive markets are the ideal in today's economy. In fact, while often looked for, they are seldom found."[4] In other words, the sort of market condition that, explicitly or implicitly, is presupposed as the ideal or the norm by the neoclassical model hardly exists. Instead there are markets dominated in one way or another by large firms, firms moreover that use their economic power to affect prices for both consumers and suppliers, market share, the price of labor, and so on.

Now it is true that economists have come to recognize the existence of what they call imperfectly competitive markets. My complaint is that, even while they do so, the model of perfect competition remains the paradigm, the "ideal" as Samuelson terms it, always lurking at the back of the whole myth of the market, the myth that the individual's desire to maximize his economic gain is the means by which the various measures in the economy, such as prices, wages, etc., are set, and which, moreover, will produce the maximum benefit to society as a whole. On the other hand, were imperfect competition recognized as the norm and the starting point of our analysis, and were factors such as power and legal or cultural norms recognized as equally important determinants of economic outcomes, then the utility of the neoclassical graphs and equations would be severely compromised — indeed the whole myth of the omnipotent market would be called into question.

Let us examine another of Samuelson's economic relations which is held to be a key concept of economic

---

[4] *Microeconomics*, p. 166.

analysis. The concept of the *marginal*, or the additional unit produced, sold or consumed, is of great importance in neoclassical economic doctrine. Marginal cost (MC), for example, "denotes the extra or additional cost of producing 1 extra unit of output." This, he says, "is one of the most important concepts in all of economics."[5] Rational firms, that is, the kind of economic actors that Samuelson and other economists presuppose, always seek to equate their marginal cost with their marginal revenue (MR), "the change in revenue that is generated by an additional unit of sales."[6] Samuelson includes a great many charts and graphs illustrating this. But let us bump up against the real world. For Samuelson blithely admits that most firms do not even bother to set their production by the MC=MR rule.

> For example, it is common practice for companies — especially ones in imperfectly competitive markets — to set prices on a "cost-plus-markup" basis.... Instead of setting prices by an MR and MC comparison, companies take the calculated average cost of a product and mark it up by adding a fixed percentage....[7]

So it turns out that "one of the most important concepts in all of economics" has hardly any application in the real world, which is characterized largely by imperfectly competitive firms largely ignoring MC, as Samuelson acknowledges. So if this is so, why go to great lengths to discuss concepts and formulas which have mostly no application to reality? Such graphs and formulas do have a purpose, however. That purpose is to fix in the minds of students the myth of the self-regulating market, so that however much they may admit that the ideal world of rational actors in perfectly

---

[5] *Microeconomics*, p. 126.
[6] *Microeconomics*, p. 175.
[7] *Microeconomics*, p. 192.

competitive markets, carefully calculating their marginal costs and revenue, hardly exists, still they will
conduct their analyses and deliver their policy advice
with such a model always subconsciously lurking at
the back of their minds.

I mentioned that Samuelson and his school assume
that individuals and firms are rational economic actors.
That is, everyone is out to maximize profit, minimize
expenses, and seek after these ends in a rational and
consistent manner. Without such an assumption the
ideal world of neoclassical graphs and equations would
vanish. But is this the real world? In the *Study Guide*
that accompanies Samuelson's text, the authors make
an interesting admission:

> In this discussion, we assume that the firm's
> objective is to *maximize profits*. Note that there are
> other perfectly reasonable objectives that firms
> might have. For example, many not-for-profit
> organizations, such as hospitals, churches, and even
> many universities, exist in a market economy; the
> goals of these firms might be to serve the community
> or provide for social welfare. In other cases, firms
> aggressively market their products and try endlessly
> to increase sales and market share, seeming to
> maximize revenues or production rather than
> profits. In some cases, CEOs of companies seem
> to be interested in maximizing their own salaries
> rather than the profitability of the enterprises that
> employ them.[8]

One wonders how many for-profit firms actually do
try to maximize profits. Either because of ignorance,
carelessness, difficulty of calculation, or other goals —
such as maximizing CEO compensation or sometimes
pride of workmanship — even occasionally because of
good will toward employees and customers, perhaps a

---

[8] Laurence Miners and Kathryn Nantz, *Study Guide for Use with
Microeconomics*, (Boston: McGraw-Hill Irwin, 2001), p. 105.

sizeable number of firms do not try to maximize profits, at least not in a sustained and careful way. Would not economic analysis better describe the actual workings of the economy if it discussed all this first and at greater length instead of adding it as a kind of afterthought? Moreover, if our culture and laws did not encourage or even mandate maximization of profits as the only rational purpose of a firm, then perhaps even fewer firms would aim at this goal.

Economists such as Samuelson seem to want to make their subject as much like physics as they can, but in dealing with a real world of men and power, they would do better to look at the many different ways in which people relate to one another and use their power, and even sometimes their good will, toward each other. The economy is not a self-regulating mechanism whose operations can be neatly captured by graphs and equations. Human motivations are many and vary widely between different times and places. Market forces, such as the desire to buy cheap and sell dear, certainly exist, but they never operate in a vacuum. They are determined and shaped by many forces, especially by their cultural context and by the legal system, whose sanctions have immense influence on economic behavior. For example, the limited liability conferred on corporations is a creation of civil law, and could be changed at any time. If corporate directors, still more shareholders, were made potentially criminally liable for misbehavior on the part of corporations, think how much this would change the behavior of corporations. In addition, raw power, exercised either directly via economic means, or indirectly via politics, greatly shapes economic outcomes, for example, as corporations strive to control legislative and regulatory bodies on behalf of their interests and profits.

It is true, of course, that the texts I am dealing with here are meant for beginners, often college freshmen, and that as students progress in the study of economics their concepts and analytic tools become more complex and sophisticated. While this is true it is not of great importance. For by treating perfect competition and rational economic actors as the "ideal," everything else is rendered an exception, an afterthought, something to be explained with constant reference to an economic world that does not exist. Moreover, why would beginners in any subject be taught a paradigm that does not accord with reality? If the real world of economic behavior is complex and is always influenced by non-economic factors, why not make that clear to students at the outset? The grasp of the simplistic formulas of neoclassical economics will do little to help students sort out and make sense of the actual economic behavior of real people. Rather it will make them more likely to attempt to fit their perception of the actual economic behavior around them into the neat formulas, graphs and equations taught to the neophyte. Hence we end up with the fact that "Many economists have struggled to accept that bubbles exist, as that is difficult to square with the idea of efficient markets." There will always be a bias in the mind of the economist toward attempting to understand economic behavior according to an ideal that does not exist.

The attempt on the part of economists to emulate the physical sciences has not helped us in our understanding of how economies actually work. Rather it has done considerable damage by serving to spread the notion that economic outcomes are in great measure determined by impersonal market forces, beyond the ability of man to shape or change. For example, the steady increase in the amount of wealth and income obtained by the richest in the United States since about 1980 is hardly an accident or the result of impersonal and competitive economic forces. It could more accurately be called a conspiracy, although a conspiracy largely conducted in public view. The changes in laws or regulations regarding taxation, labor unions, investments, the environment, and many other social and economic matters have together created a situation in which income and wealth have flowed to the richest, while the wages of everyone else have mostly remained flat or even declined. But mainstream economics tends to explain this in impersonal terms, rather than as an outcome of the use of political, economic and media power. If the study of economics is to be of benefit to the human race, instead of serving mostly as a rationalization of capitalist wealth and power, it must take account of the actualities of economic life. Economic activity does not exist in a vacuum, a vacuum in which detached rational actors interact among themselves with little reference to the rest of human affairs. It is a part of human social life and as such, subject to most of the same constraints, pressures, and cultural conditioning that characterize the life of mankind. It is impossible that it could be otherwise, for we can hardly separate neatly our decisions about economic matters from all the other choices we make.

In subsequent chapters we will consider many of the specific aspects and institutions of economic life, always keeping in mind the general principles and criticisms laid down in my two introductory chapters.

SECTION II

Special Topics

3

Economic Regulation

One of the perennial economic topics of interest is that of regulation of the economy. In fact, it often appears to be the chief area of controversy in much of our current political discourse, with one side advocating more regulation and the other side less. In this chapter we will consider both the need for economic regulation and how and by whom such regulation is best carried out.

Those who seek to reduce the amount of economic regulation often appeal, explicitly or implicitly, to the notion of a self-regulating market, that is a market operating according to what are called the laws of supply and demand, tempered only by prohibitions against force or fraud. Such a market is usually termed a *free market* and presupposes the notion discussed in the last chapter, that "through the workings of the invisible hand, those who pursue their own self-interest in a competitive economy will most effectively promote the public interest." Paul Samuelson's definition of a market is essentially that of a free market, "An arrangement whereby buyers and sellers interact to determine the prices and quantities of a commodity."[1] This kind of economy is held to be the ideal by libertarians and most supporters of neoliberal capitalism. Moreover, most neoclassical economists seem to regard it as a model, at least in the sense that it works as the organizing principle for the whole edifice of economics which they have constructed, even if they might admit that in practice it is neither wholly attainable nor necessarily even desirable.

---

[1] *Microeconomics*, p. 426.

Before asking whether such a market is a good thing or not we might note that any organized market necessarily operates with some rules, in this case with the prohibitions against force and fraud. For a truly *free* market, if we take the words literally, would be simply one of chaos: a mob fighting over some new electronic gadget in a store or marauders plundering fields or villages — this would be economic activity without any rules whatsoever, except might makes right. But of course, defenders of what are usually called free markets do not mean anything like this. So in the first instance, we see that everyone admits the need for some kinds of rules to regulate market behavior. The question is, what rules shall a market operate under and who shall make them? What kinds of misleading conduct or speech shall be termed fraud and thus forbidden, what uses of power or force prohibited? If we follow this line of argument, we can argue that no market is truly free, for some rules are always present. We might better call a so-called free market a market with a minimum of rules, where the interaction of buyers and sellers is the chief mechanism by which the market functions.

Now, is such a system a good thing? We might begin with Pope Pius XI's negative characterization of such a market in his encyclical *Quadragesimo Anno* (1931):

> Just as the unity of human society cannot be built upon "class" conflict, so the proper ordering of economic affairs cannot be left to the free play of rugged competition [*permitti libero virium certamini*]. From this source, as from a polluted spring, have proceeded all the errors of the "individualistic" school. This school, forgetful or ignorant of the social and moral aspects of economic activities, regarded these as completely free and immune from any intervention by public authority, for they would have in the market place and in unregulated competition [*in mercato seu libero competitorum certamine*] a

principle of self-direction more suitable for guiding them than any created intellect which might intervene. (no. 88)

And in another place in the same encyclical Pius wrote:

> This accumulation of power, a characteristic note of the modern economic order, is a natural result of unrestrained free competition which permits the survival of those only who are the strongest. This often means those who fight most relentlessly, who pay least heed to the dictates of conscience. (no. 107)

We can discern several distinct points made in these two quotes. First, the avowal that unregulated competition leads to the neglect of "the social and moral aspects of economic activities," together with the implication that in fact intelligent human intervention is at least sometimes a necessary corrective or supplement to market competition. We will consider below what some of the "social and moral aspects of economic activities" might be.

In the second quote the Pontiff notes that "accumulation of [economic] power...is a natural result of unrestrained free competition," and secondly, the reason for this is that "free competition...permits the survival of those only who are the strongest. This often means those who fight most relentlessly, who pay least heed to the dictates of conscience." Free competition, then, will almost always lead to economic domination because the compensating mechanisms assumed by neoclassical economics, such as the entry of new firms into the marketplace, by no means can be counted on because there is more involved than simply the application of impersonal economic laws. It is actual human beings who are market participants and economic competitors, and they will generally strive to increase their power and to obtain positions from which they can dominate others and obtain economic outcomes favorable to themselves, including erecting barriers to new competitors. They are not simply the passive tools of the forces of supply and demand as posited by the deductive model of economists, but generally they have power to take advantage of others and to fight for their own economic interests, fairly or not, and thus to influence market outcomes according to their desires.

Despite the assertion that "those who pursue their own self-interest in a competitive economy will most effectively promote the public interest," there is no reason to suppose that what we call free markets will automatically produce justice. They have no means of guaranteeing the payment of a just wage or of just prices for consumers. But neither will they even necessarily produce economic prosperity. They will very often produce masses of goods, but whether these goods will correspond to authentic human needs and serve the true cultivation of the human person and of society as a whole is another matter. Mere production of material goods does not necessarily provide well for the economic needs of a population. In the first place, this is because such markets respond to the demands of those with money, who are not usually the majority of the population. Thus basic and cheap food which the poor need and desire may not make as much profit for those who own land or the means of production as more expensive food produced for the rich will do. This can be seen most clearly when, because of free trade agreements, land which once grew modest crops for domestic use is now used for growing food for export, but food which is priced beyond the means of the domestic poor. There is no guarantee that the needs of those whose buying power is insufficient to compete with the rich will be met when the owners of the means of production direct their efforts toward those with the most money and ignore the rest.

Secondly, even for those who do command sufficient buying power to be able to influence the choices of producers and sellers, there is no guarantee that products and services offered for sale constitute contributions to the satisfaction of genuine human needs.

> If... a direct appeal is made to human instincts — while ignoring in various ways the reality of the person as intelligent and free — then *consumer attitudes and lifestyles* can be created which are objectively improper and often damaging to the person's physical and spiritual health. Of itself, an economic system does not possess criteria for correctly distinguishing new and higher forms of satisfying human needs from artificial new needs which hinder the formation of a mature personality. (*Centesimus Annus*, no. 36)

Advertising exists to sell products and does not distinguish "new and higher forms of satisfying human needs from artificial new needs which hinder the formation of a mature personality." The defenders of what we call a free market make unproved and unprovable assertions about its ability to produce goods and respond to consumer demand. But especially they like to contrast their own economic model with the real or supposed defects of other systems. Since Adam Smith the main selling point of the free market has been its alleged superiority over its rivals, rather than its inherent virtues. Some will even admit its weaknesses, but then argue that any other system is worse, and therefore we had best embrace it or we will end up with scarcity and poverty. But such arguments are for the most part special pleading which do not compare a free market with every alternative, but with those alternatives only, such as a command economy, that do have more serious defects, or with a merely theoretical abstraction which is easily condemned on paper because it does not operate according to the mechanistic model which mainstream

economic theory believes corresponds to actual existing economies. There are many ways of organizing an
economy. We are not condemned to choose between
a free market and some kind of centralized command
economy in which decision makers order the production of goods and services based on bureaucratic rules
or political priorities. There are numerous alternatives
to our present system, some better and some worse.

When mostly unrestrained competition is the main
determining factor in an economy, those who possess economic power have a constant temptation to
lower their costs by taking advantage of those with the
least economic power, generally their employees and
the public, not merely as to wages or prices, but with
regard to such external costs as pollution, the cost of
which can often be transferred to society as a whole. A
firm cannot usually cut its costs with regard to the raw
materials it buys or the utilities it needs to operate. But
as long as an abundant supply of workers is available,
labor costs can usually be lowered, even if that means
that a real home or family life for their employees
is impossible. Similarly, the costs and consequences
of pollution can be transferred to the public, if these
consequences can be hidden from public scrutiny or
justified as an unfortunate necessity.

What sort of market, then, ought we to desire, with
what kind of regulation, and who exactly is to do the
regulating? Earlier I quoted Pope Pius XI's condemnation of those who "would have in the market place and
in unregulated competition a principle of self-direction
more suitable for guiding them than any created intellect which might intervene." If so, then what "created
intellect" is to regulate the economy. Who is to under-
take this task? In the United States today it is usually
assumed that if we reject the notion of self-regulating
markets, then economic regulation must be done by
the federal government. And sometimes this is true,

only the central government can deal with certain situations. But not always or even usually will this be the case. Generally regulation can and should be done by lower bodies. In the first place the principle of subsidiarity—the principle that higher and larger bodies, including the state, should not absorb the functions and duties of lower and smaller ones—is the key to dealing successfully with socio-economic questions.[2]

There are several reasons for this, but in the first place, regulation by lower and smaller bodies meets one important objection to government regulation made by economic liberals—those known as conservatives or libertarians in the United States—which rests on the charge that government bureaucrats know little about the realities of industry and are apt to promulgate rules and standards that are abstract and too rigid. And at times there no doubt is some truth to this charge. But the answer is not to do away with regulation. No, the answer is to place regulatory power in its proper and natural place, with those actually doing the work, those who do know the realities of the industry and who themselves must bear any safety hazard. This was the approach in the medieval urban economy where economic regulation was generally left in the hands of the guilds, private organizations in the sense that they

---

[2] "It is indeed true, as history clearly shows, that owing to the change in social conditions, much that was formerly done by small bodies can nowadays be accomplished only by large organizations. Nevertheless it is a fundamental principle of social philosophy, fixed and unchangeable, that one should not withdraw from individuals and commit to the community what they can accomplish by their own enterprise and industry. So, too, it is an injustice and at the same time a grave evil and a disturbance of right order, to transfer to the larger and higher collectivity functions which can be performed and provided for by lesser and subordinate bodies." *Quadragesimo Anno*, no. 79. Note that the principle does not call for the lowest or smallest possible body to be the locus for action, rather that if something can be successfully accomplished by a lower body, then that is the appropriate level for that activity.

were not organs of government, but who nevertheless performed important governmental tasks. Let us look at a definition of medieval guilds in order better to understand their purpose and necessity.

> A guild was a federation of autonomous workshops, whose owners (the masters) normally made all decisions and established the requirements for promotion from the lower ranks (journeymen or hired helpers, and apprentices). Inner conflicts were usually minimized by a common interest in the welfare of the craft and a virtual certitude that sooner or later every proficient apprentice and industrious journeyman would become a master and share in the governance of the craft. To make sure that expectations would be fulfilled, a guild would normally forbid overtime work after dark and sometimes limit the number of dependents a master could employ; this also served to maintain substantial equality among masters and to prevent overexpansion of the craft.[3]

As a consequence of the natural function of guilds in taking care of matters of common concern, they were also the natural locus for economic regulation. The state, on the other hand, although it has the widest interest in the common good and the welfare of all of society, generally should confine itself to "directing, supervising, encouraging, restraining" the lower bodies as they go about their proper and immediate tasks.[4] Thus the government, at every level, must have a vital concern for the common good and for the institutions and practices that society uses to fulfill its needs, but most often this concern will not be exercised directly.

What then would be the proper regulatory powers of guilds? Let me begin to answer that with a quotation

---

[3] Robert S. Lopez, *The Commercial Revolution of the Middle Ages, 950–1350.* (Cambridge: Cambridge University, 1976), p. 127.
[4] Cf. *Quadragesimo Anno*, no. 80.

from Msgr. John A. Ryan, the greatest American theologian on the Church's social doctrine.

> The occupational group [guild] might be empowered by law to fix wages, interest, dividends, and prices, to determine working conditions, to adjust industrial disputes, and to carry on whatever economic planning was thought feasible. All the groups in the several concerns of an industry could be federated into a national council for the whole industry. There could also be a federation of all the industries of the nation. The occupational groups, whether local or national, would enjoy power and authority over industrial matters coming within their competence. This would be genuine self-government in industry.
>
> Of course, the occupational groups would not be entirely independent of the government. No economic group, whether of capitalists or laborers, or of both in combination, can be trusted with unlimited power to fix their own profits and remuneration. While allowing to the occupational groups the largest measure of reasonable freedom in the management of their own affairs, the State, says Pius XI, should perform the tasks which belong to it and which it alone can effectively accomplish, namely, those of "directing, watching, stimulating, and restraining, as circumstances suggest or necessity demands...."[5]

In other words, the chief function of the guilds is to oversee a particular trade or industry so that its prices and wages are fair, its products are well-made and are produced in such a manner as not to harm either the worker or the larger physical environment, and there is an approximate equivalence between the number of workers in a particular trade and the public's genuine need for their product or service, so that there will be steady work for all in the trade or industry. In

---

[5] *Distributive Justice* (New York: Macmillan, 3rd ed., 1942), pp. 340–41.

addition, guilds would probably take on many of the subsidiary functions now performed by government or others, e.g., pensions and health insurance, owning their own industrial banks or credit unions to provide financial services to guild members, especially financing for those starting out in the field, and they would act as trade associations to represent the trade to outside interested parties, such as the government, other guilds whose members serve as suppliers or customers, etc. Moreover, one of the most important benefits of the presence of guilds in an economy may well be the promotion of social charity, of that fraternal love of neighbor without which individuals and entire societies will fall more and more into selfish behavior, despite how just or perfect their institutions and legal codes may be.[6]

It will be clear from the above that in the exercise of all these tasks guild members must always seek more than just their own well-being. As Pope Pius XI wrote, " . . . it is easy to conclude that in these associations the common interest of the whole 'group' must predominate: and among these interests the most important is the directing of the activities of the group to the common good."[7] In other words, and as I have already mentioned, a guild must not aim simply at its own good, but realize that all economic activity exists for the sake of the common good. If an industry is flourishing but supplying the public with shoddy or useless goods

---

[6] Cf. Pius XI, *Quadragesimo Anno*, nos. 88, 137; John Paul II, *Centesimus Annus*, no. 10.

[7] *Quadragesimo Anno*, no. 85. Pius' classic statement of the nature and functions of guilds is in *Quadragesimo Anno*, nos. 81 to 87. Although Pius XI and Pius XII spoke of guilds or occupational groups more frequently than have more recent popes, it is not true that there are no references to such institutions in papal social teaching after Pius XII. See John XXIII, *Mater et Magistra*, no. 37, and nos. 65–67, 84, 86–90 and 100. Also John Paul II, *Laborem Exercens*, nos. 14 and 20, and *Centesimus Annus*, nos. 7, 13, 43, 48.

or polluting the environment, then that industry is not
fulfilling its task. It is more like a criminal syndicate
which lives by taking advantage of society. Therefore
guilds must be concerned not only with obvious matters affecting the common good, such as product quality
and fair prices, but be willing to play a constructive role
in the economy and even in society at large.

What of the internal structures of guilds or their
relations with one another and with outside parties,
especially the government, either local or central? The
internal structure of a guild could be comparatively
simple, for only in large firms will there be a complex
structure of owners, managers and workers who must
all receive fair representation in the guild's governance.
Except in such cases, owners of small productive property would be the primary members of a guild, but
there would have to be some way of giving a voice to
those in apprenticeship or other training programs, as
well as to journeymen, that is, those who had com-
pleted their training and were working for wages while
gaining experience and capital for setting up their own
shop or workshop or farm. Also, we must allow for
the possibility that there would be some who would
prefer to continue as journeymen throughout their
lives, having no desire to establish their own businesses.
But in any case, these journeymen would also be guild
members, who must have some representation in the
governance of the guild.

Depending on various factors such as the industry
in question, the technology employed, the source of
raw materials, etc., a guild could have its chief locus of
activities in one particular city or district, or in a larger
regional or national sphere. In many cases industries
would need to coordinate on a regional or national
level, for example, to negotiate regional contracts for
the purchase of raw materials or machinery. These
federations of local guilds might also be the first place

in which disputes between guilds were adjudicated, with appeal to civil courts as a last resort.

It is important to emphasize the point that guilds are not voluntary associations. That is, if one wishes to exercise a certain trade or profession, he will be obliged to become and remain a member of the appropriate guild, and will be subject to its rules, which of course will be formulated democratically by the guild members themselves. This is hardly an infringement on our legitimate freedom, for our economic freedom exists so that we can make a decent living for ourselves and our families, not so that we can amass riches beyond our needs. For as in G. K. Chesterton's remark that I have already quoted, the institution of private property no more implies the right to unlimited property than the institution of marriage implies the right to unlimited wives.

With regard to relations with the government, we must remember that the guilds will be legal persons in their own right.

> In legal language the vocational group would be designated as a corporation or a syndicate. It would in some manner be regarded as a moral person capable of assuming responsibility for its corporate actions and of representing the interests of its members. The State would have to see that the corporation fulfills the social function wherefor it exists and in return enjoys the social advantages, material and cultural, which the general condition of society warrants and should make available for all. Within the corporation, since there would be no one possessing a disproportionate power, all matters could be settled on a democratic basis.[8]

In short, with its stable legal status a guild would be able to represent the interests of the trade or profession

---

[8] Charles P. Bruehl, *The Pope's Plan for Social Reconstruction: A Commentary on the Social Encyclicals of Pius XI* (New York: Devin-Adair, 1939), pp. 247–48.

as a whole, yet always aware that those interests were subordinate to the overall interests of society, both economic and otherwise. A reasonable prosperity would of course be sought, but a prosperity which respected the rights and needs of other guilds and their members, of the consuming public, and of the overall economic, cultural and even spiritual state and needs of the locality or region. No conception of guilds should attempt to isolate their economic aspects from the general welfare of society, and even from man's true destiny to live with God forever in heaven.

Economic regulation, then, for the sake of the common good, is best carried out by intermediate groups, guilds or occupational groups as they are often called. This approach renders moot much of the economic debate in today's capitalist world where such entities as guilds are hardly known. Our often sterile debate about regulation is simply undercut by the approach advocated here.

4

Money and
Token Wealth

*Productions are always bought by productions,
or by services; money is only the medium by
which the exchange is effected.*

—David Ricardo[1]

I

I
t should not need too much consideration to show
that our economic life, and as a result, our theoretical discussions about economics, ought to be
chiefly about real *things*, not about their surrogates or
tokens, such as money or stock certificates. Yet obviously in any economy above a primitive level, these
surrogates must play an important role, for exchange
by barter is no longer possible or at least convenient in
most cases. But if it is the case that in the end it is real
things that matter, not tokens, then exchange by barter
becomes, to pardon the expression, the gold standard
of real economic exchange, for the more an economy
must work by means of the exchange of surrogates or
tokens of real wealth, the more there is an opportunity for manipulation, opening the way to every sort
of chicanery, or even just to complications that arise
from no one's fault but from the complexity of the
system of exchange.

But in fact, we do frequently confuse these two
things, real wealth and mere surrogates. The rise and
fall of the stock market, for example, neither adds nor

---

[1] *The Principles of Political Economy and Taxation* (London: J. M.
Dent, [1817] 1933), p. 194.

subtracts any real wealth from the country, but almost everyone sees this as somehow not only a sign but even a cause of our national economic health. However when we realize that it is things rather than surrogates that matter, then we will take whatever steps are necessary to subordinate financial markets to serve the provision of real goods, rather than to subject the production of real wealth to the power of those who spend their days trading in tokens.

Fr. Vincent McNabb gives an interesting example that occurred during the hyper-inflation in Germany in the early 1920s, when the value of the German mark had fallen to fantastically low levels. Quoting a newspaper report from October 1924, Fr. McNabb relates that at Frankfurt-am-Main farmers would not sell their potatoes, "the chief article of food of the working classes, because they do not consider it worth the trouble to burden themselves with more paper marks. The authorities propose to offer them ammonia from the gas-works in exchange for potatoes."[2] In other words, here are two real economic goods, potatoes, and ammonia gas. Both are needed and both can be exchanged. But a currency that has somehow taken on a life of its own stands between these two real goods and makes exchanges nearly impossible. By a temporary return to barter, however, the German authorities had by-passed the financial arrangements and made real economic life possible. Of course, barter is not a sensible way to run a complex economy in normal times, but this example strikingly illustrates that it is real wealth which we need, and that whenever surrogates for such wealth get in the way of production and exchange, then the management of such tokens has gone askew. If the New York Stock Exchange says we are poor because of a fall in the value of stocks, we ought to count the number of farms and cows and steel plants we have,

---

[2] *The Church and the Land* (Norfolk: IHS Press [1925] 2003), p. 160.

let alone those who can work these farms or factories, and ask whether the stock exchange has the power to add or subtract one bit of real wealth from the country.

I now offer what I call an economic fable, designed not to narrate the actual historical invention of money, but to illustrate its essential nature. This is a *logical*, not historical, account of the origin and development of money.

The first sorts of exchanges would necessarily have been by barter. One person had wheat, another shoes, another was a carpenter, another a miller. If the farmer needed shoes and the shoemaker wheat, then an exchange was easy. But it surely must happen that the shoemaker needed wheat at a time when the farmer did not need shoes. Perhaps then the shoemaker had something else to trade. But if not, he could give the farmer a slip, good for a certain amount of shoes, redeemable whenever the farmer needed shoes. A slip would be an IOU. Yet these slips or scrip could be exchanged with third parties too. Suppose the farmer mentioned above needed some carpentry work done, yet the carpenter did not need any wheat at that time. The farmer could give the carpenter the scrip from the shoemaker as payment, and similarly this scrip could be traded by the carpenter with someone else, and so on. It is an item of value because it represents a claim on a product, namely shoes.

It would soon be convenient for all the producers to issue this scrip to avoid the necessity of immediate product exchange (barter) when no product was needed by one of the parties to a transaction.

Concomitantly, a process of standardization of value would necessarily be going on. There would emerge a rough consensus as to how much wheat was worth so many shoes, so much carpentry work, etc. Even though individuals might differ in their estimate of the value of some items, at least for necessities and other things of general use the community would gradually form a rough common estimation of comparative value.[3] So as the use of these slips became general, many of them would circulate around the community, each one good for a certain product or service, yet standing in some quantitative relation one to another. For example, if someone bought a pair of shoes he would expect to pay for it with scrip of equivalent worth, say, a scrip worth one bushel of wheat. Or if he had a house built, he would pay for it with a scrip for shoes, clothes, wheat or what have you, yet standing in some more or less fixed quantitative relationship with the worth of the building materials and work.

The next step would be for each producer no longer to indicate a particular product on his scrip, but simply some unit of value. This would require that some particular product be accepted as a standard for determining value, say wheat. If, for example, it had become the practice for a pair of shoes to equal one bushel of wheat, then the shoemaker might begin marking his scrip simply with the notation One Unit, and the farmer likewise. Other producers who made more costly items could indicate larger values on their scrip, and so on. So the shoemaker would produce scrip which in a sense represented a claim on a future pair of shoes, but since they named no particular product or service could be spent on any product or service, and in this way become a general claim for any economic good or service. With this you have now established a complete system of money.

Some points need to be noted. What "backs" this pure paper money? In one sense it is backed by the faith

---

[3] Of course this would need to be based on other factors as well, including scarcity and the cost of production, and in fact these would usually be taken into account. In different communities the value of products might be estimated differently depending on such factors, e.g., wine in a wine-producing country would probably receive a lower price than wine in a country where it would need to be imported from a distance.

of the particular community that their scrip money will be accepted for the goods they need. In another sense of "back," the money is backed by the economic power of the community, the ability of the community to produce the goods and services its people need to live. The money in fact is a claim on some economically valuable good or service, a kind of IOU. Does the money itself represent an addition to the wealth of the community? No. If it did, each producer could cease to practice his trade and begin writing money-slips all day long instead. The only things of economic value are products, services or land. The scrip just enables these items to change hands more easily, aids in standardizing their relative worth and in allowing economic values to be stored for future use, since it is easier to keep a quantity of scrip than of some actual product.

The money system is now set up. Previously, before the slips of paper had become divorced from a particular product or service, they were made by each individual economic producer whenever he needed to buy something for which he could not at the time barter; and they stood in some relation to his existing supply of goods or to his ability to create new goods, for if the shoemaker, for example, instead of making shoes, made slips of paper supposedly redeemable for shoes, with no actual stock of shoes on hand or any intention to make shoes, soon people would find this out, and not accept his slips. So he could not make more slips than he had shoes in stock, or could produce within a reasonable time. But when the slips no longer represent a particular product and simply state an economic unit of value, redeemable for anything costing that much, who is to issue the money, and how much are they to issue?

First, how much? The answer is implied in what I said above. If the money is in units of economic value, and this economic value is in reference to available products or services, then the amount of money must keep pace with the amount of goods and services available, unless the value of the money is to change. Money is simply a surrogate for real economic goods and services. As the amount of economic activity increases or decreases, the money supply should roughly keep pace with that increase or decrease.

Who is to issue the money? This also is suggested by our discussion. It is the community, or at least the economically active portion of the community, who logically should issue money, just as previously it was the economically active members of society who issued their individual scrip. But, concretely, who would this be? There is more than one possible answer to that, it seems to me. One obvious choice is the guardian of the temporal common good, that is, the government. Another possible, and probably better, candidate would be the federation of all guilds (occupational groups), working via a financial institution set up and supervised by this federation with ultimate supervision by the state, as required.

In the economies of today, however, money is largely created in a very different manner, although this is hardly known by much of the public. Today it is the private banking system that creates the vast majority of a nation's money supply, and it does so as debt. The following account will make this clear.

> An individual banker might say that his bank cannot create or destroy money. This is true insofar as an individual bank is concerned. But it is not true of our commercial banking system as a whole. Most of the monetary supply is created by the banking system and is withdrawn from the economy when it is not needed.
>
> The ability of the commercial banking system to create money is based on the *fractional reserve* banking method. The basic business of a commercial

bank is to accept deposits, most of which are in turn loaned to other customers at interest. The bank makes most of its income from this interest. It can loan money deposited by some of its customers because it knows from long experience that all its depositors are not likely to want to withdraw all their funds at the same time. In other words, it is only necessary that a bank keep a fractional amount of its deposits on reserve in the form of cash to meet its daily needs.

Let us assume that banks feel that they must keep, or that they are legally required to keep, 20 per cent of all their deposits on hand as a reserve. Then, let us trace what may happen if you deposit $1,000 in a bank. This deposit increases the bank's cash on hand by $1,000. Of this amount, it must keep $200 in reserve, but it can loan $800 to someone else. Assume that the person borrowing the $800 now deposits all of this in a second bank. That bank's deposits increase by $800, of which it can loan $640. If this borrowed $640 is in turn deposited in a third bank, that bank can loan $512. And so it can go, throughout the banking system. All of this may be done by checks; no currency or coins need be involved.

Note, however, that you still have a deposit of $1,000 in your bank. Also, the three borrowers have deposits in other banks in the amounts of $800, $640, and $512, respectively. Each of you can write checks against your deposits. Your original $1,000 has now been expanded to $2,952 in actual buying power — or $1,952 dollars in new deposit money has been created.[4]

Thus in today's economies money creation has largely been turned over to private profit-making entities who create money, use it to make loans, and then receive interest on it. But this is totally unnecessary

[4] Roy J. Sampson and Thomas W. Calmus, *Economics: Concepts, Applications, Analysis* (Boston: Houghton Mifflin, 1974), pp. 75–76.

and in fact represents a clear case of usury or unjust interest taking. In the hypothetical system sketched above the private banking system plays no such role in money creation, for there is no reason for it to do so. The money-creating role of banks is economically unnecessary, and in fact a kind of tax and blight on the community, since all the money created by the banking system comes into being as debt and must be repaid with interest.

Although there is no need for a private banking system which purports to create wealth or money as debt, obviously some kind of financial institutions are necessary. Above I suggested a financial institution controlled by the various occupational groups (guilds) of a country. In this way the financial system would be firmly subordinated to the actual productive economy, and there is less likelihood that the financial system would take on a life of its own to the detriment of the real economy. Clearly, just as the entire economy is or should be at the service of human life, so the financial system exists to serve the productive economy, i.e., the individuals and organizations that produce real goods and services. If this is so, then it is the latter that should control the banks and not *vice versa*. Thus all banks for businesses should be cooperatives controlled by occupational groups, or perhaps each occupational group would have its own bank. Financial institutions for individual consumer needs should be cooperative institutions of individuals, such as credit unions are today.

Note also that there is no logical role for gold or any other commodity as money. The desire for commodity money often represents a confusion about the nature of money, as if money itself were to have value, and not simply be a claim on real economic goods and services. In view, however, of a widespread feeling that money must be "backed" by some precious metal, usually gold, i.e., that unless paper money circulating has an equivalent of gold sitting in some vault, which can at least theoretically be exchanged for it, the paper money is in reality worthless (what is called fiat money), a few more comments are in order.

Consider our hypothetical economy described above. Suppose that the farmer discovered a gold mine on his property, and instead of growing crops he mined the gold and made it into coins. Well, gold is useful for certain industrial processes and for jewelry. For these purposes the gold would indeed be an addition to the wealth of the community and could be correctly exchanged for the paper money of the commonwealth. But what of the gold as money? Does it constitute anything of economic value? No, for consider that a large influx of gold would have exactly the same effect as a large influx of paper money, i.e., to make money worth less and to drive prices up, which is the same thing. As I said, the amount of money in circulation should have a proportionate relationship with the amount of economic goods available in the society, the amount of goods, services and land. But if the money supply is increased by printing large amounts of paper currency without a corresponding increase in economic goods, inflation will result. But why is gold different? The same thing would happen, since the gold is not really an addition to the wealth of the community, save for the small amount useful for decorative or industrial purposes.

II

We have looked at money and money creation, both in their essential aspects and as used and practiced today. This next section will sketch a notable instance of how our tendency to regard mere token or surrogates as real wealth has led to a remarkable case, namely, the conversion of what was originally a real economic good into a token. This illustrates again the ability of our economy and of our economics to grossly misunderstand

and pervert the real purposes of the production and exchange of goods.

The human race has always grown or otherwise gathered food, and there has probably always existed some kinds of exchange. But the growing or obtaining of food and the exchange of one desired object for another was always seen as a subordinate part of the life of the human race. Obtaining food was for the sake of living, exchange was for the sake of living better. But today this common-sense relationship of means and ends is very often perverted. Now production is for the sake of exchange, and in turn it becomes subordinated to more exotic financial practices. This is because the imperative is always more sales, more profit, more speculative ways of making money, without any inherent limit or even a notion of what all this activity is for, except for the enrichment of those who own or control the economic processes. The separation of ownership from work creates a class of individuals who are removed from the production of useful objects and who regard the objects produced as primarily commodities to be sold, rather than useful goods to be consumed. Hence the imperative for more sales, ever increasing profits and market share, regardless of demand, because there is no natural limit, no end for which one is striving and with which, when obtained, one is satisfied. Let us look at the interesting example of the futures market in grain to see how the exchange of real economic goods was made into a purely speculative operation of token exchange.

In his book, *Nature's Metropolis: Chicago and the Great West*,[5] William Cronon discusses how the grain trade gave rise to the futures' market in agricultural products. This account shows the absurdity of economic activity divorced from any rational end, and eventually even from a real product. As long as something makes

---

[5] (New York: W. W. Norton, 1991).

money for those who own or control it, our economy today cares nothing for whether the activity actually contributes anything toward meeting mankind's real needs for goods and services.

Originally, as has generally been the case with mankind, grain grown on the prairies of Illinois and neighboring states was a means of feeding the farmer, his family and his neighbors. But as it became a item to be shipped and sold, and eventually turned into a commodity future at the Chicago Board of Trade, we can see the transformation of a human and natural object into the abstraction of a commodity, something regarded as merely a means of profit.

A certain amount of grain trading and shipping existed from the early nineteenth century using water transportation. But this was slow and awkward and did not reach every place. Before there could be a transformation in the trade in grain, there had to be a more efficient means of transportation. This was provided by the railroads, which were built mostly to facilitate the capitalist imperative to totally commercialize every aspect of life. If people had thought of grain as primarily a food to be consumed pretty much where it was grown, then the huge railroad network of the Mid-West would probably never have come into existence, since the existing modest means of transportation would have sufficed. Thus to implement the transformation of wheat from a food into a commodity, the railway system first had to exist. The building of the railroad network transformed not only the buying and selling of food, but the environment, both natural and cultural of the region and the nation. Thus, both building upon and transforming the human vice of greed, the new type of economic thinking powerfully shaped the entire culture and violently captured such pre-capitalist aspects of society as food production and local exchange and bent them to its purposes.

The existence of the railroad network enabled farmers to conceive of themselves not as growers of food for consumption but as producers of a commodity. Grain was shipped via the railroads to Chicago where it was held in large grain elevators for eventual shipment to the East coast. Originally the ownership of any particular sack of grain deposited in an elevator was retained by the farmer who harvested it. But naturally sacks of grain differed from each other significantly in quality. The storage of these sacks in grain elevators created a problem: "elevator operators began objecting to keeping small quantities of different owners' grain in separate bins that were only partially filled.... To avoid that..., they sought to mix grain in common bins."[6] To carry this out required some system of grain standardization or grading. After such a system was created it became possible for the elevator owners to contract for sale of a certain quantity of a certain grade of wheat, with no reference to any particular sack of wheat actually existing anywhere. And because of the ever-changing price of grain, sellers and buyers soon realized that they could essentially bet against the future price by contracting in the present for sale or purchase of a definite quantity of grain at some future date, hoping that the price would increase or decrease to their benefit by the time of the actual sale. Ultimately this created the final absurdity:

> ... futures contracts [which] were essentially interchangeable and could be bought and sold quite independently of the physical grain....
>
> Moreover, the seller ... did not necessarily even have to deliver grain on the day it fell due. As long as the buyer was willing, the two could settle their transaction by simply exchanging the difference between the grain's contracted price and its market price when the contract expired....

---

[6] Cronon, *Nature's Metropolis*, p. 114.

> [They] could complete their transaction with-
> out any grain ever changing hands. . . . The futures
> market was a market not in grain but in the *price* of
> grain. . . . [O]ne bought and sold not wheat or corn
> or oats but the *prices* of those goods as they would
> exist at a future time. Speculators made and lost
> money by selling each other legally binding fore-
> casts of how much grain prices would rise or fall.[7]

Grain went from being a means for feeding the population of farmers and others who lived nearby, to
being centrally stored in bins in Chicago and shipped
throughout the Northeast United States and into
Canada, into being merely a symbol, but nevertheless a symbol that enabled speculators to engage in
exchange. The contracts themselves have become a
commodity to be bought and sold, but the contracts
now had no necessary connection with any object of
real economic value.

Despite the claim to be the only economic system
that can produce sufficient goods to satisfy mankind's
needs, our capitalist economy is really not interested
in production at all, except as that can serve sales. It
is interested in moneymaking, to be sure, but money-
making by nearly any means that one can concoct. It
might seem obvious, for example, that the financial
sector would be a modest adjunct of the more primary
economic activities of production or even exchange,
necessary and helpful, but always subordinate. But
frequently someone can make more money by manipulation of surrogates for real wealth or by a merger or
buyout, which often results in a *decrease* in real economic activity, than by actual production.

It should be obvious that mankind's economic
activity exists to serve our need for external goods
and services. Thus economic activity must always be
subordinate to the genuine needs and interests of

---

[7] *Nature's Metropolis*, p. 125.

humanity. But when economic activity is seen as basically a means of getting rich by almost any method, it is apt to become entirely divorced from meeting real economic needs. The economy becomes essentially a private playground for those with enough skill or money to manipulate it in their favor. Pope Pius XI wrote with regard to such types of economic manipulation, "A stern insistence on the moral law, enforced with vigor by civil authority, could have dispelled or perhaps averted these enormous evils" (*Quadragesimo Anno*, no. 133). But this is too rarely the case in a commercial society, where indeed "society itself becomes an 'adjunct' of the market."[8]

III

Although the question of usury does not fit perfectly into a chapter on money, it seemed the most appropriate place to put it, since usury almost always does involve money, though strictly speaking it could involve the loan of any good which is consumed in its use, such as food or drink, in which "the obligation is imposed upon the borrower to restore to the lender, not the identical thing loaned, but its equivalent—that is, another thing of the same kind, quality, and value.... "[9] In such a case the lender undergoes no risk simply by virtue of the loan contract, since he will receive an undamaged equivalent of what he has loaned.

I think it might surprise many readers that usury in its classic definition does not mean charging excessive interest on a loan, not even on a loan for consumption purposes. It involves charging *any* interest on a loan *simply because of the existence of a loan contract*. A full

---

[8] Ellen Meiksins Wood, "From Opportunity to Imperative: the History of the Market," *Monthly Review*, vol. 46, no. 3, July–August 1994, p. 20. She is summarizing the ideas of Karl Polany's book, *The Great Transformation* (Boston: Beacon Press, 1957).
[9] William C. Morey, *Outlines of Roman Law*. (New York: G. P. Putman's, 2nd ed., 1914), p. 356.

statement of this understanding of usury was set forth in the 1745 encyclical of Pope Benedict XIV, *Vix Pervenit*.

> The nature of the sin called usury has its proper place and origin in a loan contract. This financial contract between consenting parties demands, by its very nature, that one return to another only as much as he has received. The sin rests on the fact that sometimes the creditor desires more than he has given. Therefore he contends some gain is owned him beyond that which he loaned, but any gain which exceeds the amount he gave is illicit and usurious.
>
> One cannot condone the sin of usury by arguing that the gain is not great or excessive, but rather moderate or small; neither can it be condoned by arguing that the borrower is rich; nor even by arguing that the money borrowed is not left idle, but is spent usefully, either to increase one's fortune . . . or to engage in business transactions. The law governing loans consists necessarily in the equality of what is given and returned; once the equality has been established, whoever demands more than that violates the terms of the loan. . . .

Although this might seem like an insane point of view today, consider how interest charges are in fact justified. "Interest is the payment made for the use of money,"[10] writes Paul Samuelson. In an earlier version of his textbook, Samuelson made the following statement:

> Let us make the realistic assumption that when I borrow money from you, my purpose is not to hold onto the cash: instead, I use the borrowed cash to buy capital goods . . . to create a net product over and above their replacement cost. Therefore, if I did not pay you interest, I should really be cheating you out of the return that you could get by putting your own money directly into such productive investment projects![11]

---

[10] Samuelson, *Macroeconomics*, p. 161.
[11] *Economics* (New York: McGraw-Hill, 9th ed., 1973), p. 603.

Note that Samuelson's justification for interest is that the lender could himself invest his money in some profitable enterprise, and that therefore interest is justified since he is loaning the money instead and forgoing that opportunity for gain. But if in any particular case there were no opportunities to put "your own money directly into such productive projects," then Samuelson's justification for interest collapses. And in the simpler economies of the ancient and early medieval worlds, one could not count on such opportunities being always at hand. Sometimes if a lender did not loan out his money it would simply sit in some vault, due to lack of any investment opportunity. In such a circumstance charging interest on a loan was unjustified, which is all that is meant when Benedict XIV says that "any gain which exceeds the amount [the lender] gave is illicit and usurious." But note what follows immediately in the next paragraph.

> By these remarks, however, We do not deny that at times together with the loan contract certain other titles — which are not at all intrinsic to the contract — may run parallel with it. From these other titles, entirely just and legitimate reasons arise to demand something over and above the amount due on the contract.

There do exist titles which permit interest, and when, as in our economy, the opportunity to make productive investments always exists, then for someone prepared to take advantage of such investment opportunities, the charging of interest for a loan is legitimate.[12] This is the justification for the medieval title to interest known as *lucrum cessans*, one of a handful of titles which in certain circumstances did permit charging interest. But in an

---

[12] But note that this does not justify simply any rate of interest, however high. A legitimate rate of interest must bear some relationship to the normal level of profits otherwise obtainable in any particular economy.

economy where such opportunities are missing or rare, or even today for someone unprepared or unwilling to take advantage of such opportunities, it is clear that no one is cheating the lender out of anything by not paying him interest, for if he had not made the loan, then the money would have simply sat idle. Pope Benedict was addressing the question of lending and interest absolutely speaking, and thus his remarks are correct, namely, that while in itself a "financial contract between consenting parties demands, by its very nature, that one return to another only as much as he has received," and that "any gain which exceeds the amount he gave is illicit and usurious," nevertheless it is still the case that "at times together with the loan contract certain other titles — which are not at all intrinsic to the contract — may run parallel with it," and that from these other titles "entirely just and legitimate reasons arise to demand something over and above the amount due on the contract." The fact that today such other titles always or nearly always exist, does not mean that the classic understanding of usury is wrong or outdated, simply that what was once an exceptional circumstance has become ordinary.[13]

---

[13] For a fuller discussion of usury, including the historical development of the Church's teaching, see my *An Economics of Justice and Charity* (Angelico Press, 2017), pp. 105–130, and *Money, Markets and Morals* (En Route Books & Media, 2024), pp. 15–34.

5

Buying, Selling
and Prices

In my chapter on money we saw that as a monetary system develops, prices among different items
would begin to be standardized by the common
estimation of the community. In the Middle Ages this
common estimation or *communis aestimatio* was held
to be the correct way of determining a just price, and
although as a way of arriving at prices today this might
seem like a quaint throwback to the Middle Ages, actually it is not entirely alien to our own economy. We
assume a rough determination of prices by just such a
common estimation. If one were to enter a supermarket
and find that a can of beans cost $1000 or that the nice
new car on the dealer's lot was priced at only $59.95,
things would seem out of kilter indeed. We do implicitly price items by a kind of common estimation, not
always or for every item perhaps, but for the majority
of them, at least for items in common use.

In this chapter, however, I will be chiefly concerned
with the teaching of St. Thomas Aquinas on some particular moral questions that concern buying and selling. After reviewing Thomas' teaching on these points
we will consider some of its applications to today's
economies.

In the *Summa Theologiae* II-II, St. Thomas devotes
two questions to unjust acts which are committed in
buying and selling or lending. The first of these questions (q. 77), divided into four articles, deals with fraud
in the broad sense (*fraudulentia*), while the second (q.
78) concerns usury. A study of these questions reveals

important differences not only between St. Thomas' teaching on injustices committed in economic life and the ethical attitudes common today, but differences in basic evaluations of the place of commerce in society. In order to make this clear, I will look at the first question, no. 77, setting forth first what Aquinas taught and then contrasting it with commerce and business ethics as these exist in a capitalist society.

The first article of question 77 is, Whether someone can licitly sell something for more than it is worth? As is usual, St. Thomas first brings up some objections to his own opinion, which he will answer later on. The first is that civil law permits the buyer and seller to "deceive each other" and buy or sell for less or more than something is worth. The second is that common opinion endorses the idea of buying cheap and selling dear. (I omit his third objection, which deals with friends giving each other gifts.)

After offering the objections, Thomas gives his own considered opinion. He first briefly notes that to deceive a buyer in order to sell something for more than the just price is altogether sinful. But then he turns to the main question, where there is no actual deceit involved. In that case, he says, it is also wrong to sell something for more than it is worth: "to sell something more dearly than it is worth, or buy it more cheaply, in itself is unjust and illicit." But he instances an exception, the case where a buyer might need or want something greatly while the seller would be especially hurt by its loss. In such a case the seller can charge a premium since he may charge for the damage he will receive by selling the item as well as for its value. But note that Aquinas is not talking about something such as price gouging following a natural disaster. His statement applies only when the buyer will suffer harm (*detrimentum* or *damnum*) by its loss. St. Thomas specifically says that a seller may not charge a buyer such a premium price unless he will suffer particular damage by selling it.

Then he proceeds to deal with the objections that were raised. To the first, that civil law permits buying cheap and selling dear, Thomas' answer is revealing. He states that human law must permit much that divine law will punish, but he also notes that civil law will demand restitution if the price deviates excessively from the just price, "*ultra dimidiam justi pretii quantitatem*," i.e., more than half again as much as the just price. St. Thomas notes, however, that a just price cannot be calculated with mathematical exactness, but is a "certain estimate, so that a small addition or subtraction does not seem to remove the equivalence of justice." With the second objection, that common usage allows such buying and selling, he simply states that "that common desire [to sell dear and buy cheap] is not natural, but is a vice, and therefore common to many who walk on the broad way of vices."

Let us then go on to St. Thomas's second article, Whether a sale is rendered illicit on account of a defect in the thing sold? He brings up three initial objections to the opinion. (I omit the first objection, which deals with goods whose appearances or qualities may have been altered by alchemy, as well as with the second, which deals with different measures being used in different localities.) The third objection is that it is unreasonable to expect a seller to be aware of all the defects in the thing he is selling, since "great knowledge is required which is lacking to most sellers."

Thomas then gives his opinion, which is that whether a defect arises from the quality or the quantity of the thing sold, a seller who knowingly misrepresents what he sells sins and is bound to restitution, as likewise a buyer sins and is bound to restitution if he purchases something for a lesser price than it is worth because the seller out of ignorance is not aware of its true value.

And although a seller or buyer who out of ignorance charges or pays an unjust price does not sin, if he later discovers his error, he is then bound to restitution.

His reply to the third objection is simply that one does not expect a seller to know about the "hidden qualities" of the thing to be sold, but "those only by means of which it is rendered apt for human uses," such as whether a horse is strong or runs well, which "a seller and buyer are easily able to know."

Then in his third article Aquinas asks, Whether a seller is obliged to reveal the defect of a thing sold? The first objection argues that since the seller does not compel a buyer to buy something, and is not required to examine the buyer's decision to buy, therefore he may also assume the buyer's due diligence in examining the quality of the thing sold. The second objection states that it would be foolish for a seller to hinder a sale by pointing out a defect in the thing to be sold, quoting Cicero to the effect that it would be absurd for someone to advertise a house infested with pests for sale. (I omit objection three which deals with one's obligation to offer counsel or moral advice to someone else.) Then objection four argues that if a seller is not bound to reveal information he has about an impending drop in the price of a good (which usually would cause his own price to drop immediately), then neither is he bound to reveal defects in the merchandise to be sold which would likewise result in lowering the price.

Thomas answers with his own opinion, which is that a seller is bound to reveal faults which either make the item less valuable and would therefore lower its price, or defects which would result in some harm to the buyer. However, if the seller has already discounted the item on account of its defects, he is not necessarily bound to mention those defects if they are obvious, since in that case the buyer might demand an even greater discount.

Thomas replies to the first objection that a buyer cannot judge the quality of something if its defects are hidden, so that the comparison alleged is invalid. As for the second objection, no one is bound to advertise something for sale mentioning only its defects, since the item may well have some good qualities as well. Then lastly, he answers the fourth objection, saying that a *future* event which will cause a fall (or rise) in prices is different from a present condition which does the same thing, i.e., that in strict justice one is not bound to reveal a future probable drop in price, but if a seller did give that information, or discounted his price, "he would be of very abundant virtue."

Then we come to the last article in question 77, Whether it is licit by engaging in business (*negotiando*) to sell something at a higher price than was paid for it? There are three objections adduced. (I omit the first and third objections which are basically arguments from the authority of certain Fathers of the Church.) The second objection argues that anyone who by his commercial activity sells a thing for more than he paid for it, necessarily either buys it for less than it is worth or sells it for more, and thus commits a sin.

In his reply Thomas distinguishes between various kinds of commercial activity. In the first place he mentions a "natural and necessary" sort "on account of necessities of life," and such exchange properly pertains not to businessmen [*negotiatores*] but to "*oeconomicos vel politicos*," i.e., to those who have some duty concerned with the welfare of the household or the political community, and this sort is praiseworthy. Then there is the kind of commerce engaged in for seeking gain, and this kind "is justly blamed because in itself it serves gain." But although gain in itself does not "imply anything morally good (*honestum*) or necessary, neither is it vicious or contrary to virtue in itself," provided it is done for a good end "and thus commerce is made licit."

Thus gain may be sought moderately for the support of one's household or to help the poor or to provide for the common good, and the gain sought is simply a payment for one's labor (*stipendium laboris*).

In his reply to objection two Thomas notes that someone can licitly sell something for more than he paid for it if he made improvements in the item or because its price was higher on account of being exported to some other place or on account of the passage of time or on account of the risk he had in taking it to another place.

I think that anyone who compares the business ethics of St. Thomas with those of today will be struck not only by the differences at specific points — e.g., not taking advantage of a buyer's ignorance — but on the whole approach to commercial life. But let us first look at some of the specific points before we raise more general considerations. At the very outset we are told that it is wrong to sell something for more than it is worth or to buy it for less than it is worth. This is surely one of the cardinal points at which modern economic thought is opposed to that of St. Thomas. For economics, as it has developed according to the spirit of capitalism, would reply not so much that Thomas' answer is wrong, but that the question itself is absurd. The phrase, "more than it is worth" is meaningless. Prices are determined by a quasi-mechanical process which can be graphed in the familiar manner of neoclassical economics. It is true that under a monopoly or other kinds of imperfect competition, firms can charge more than what economists consider the norm of marginal cost, still in the end something is worth whatever a buyer and a seller can agree on. No one forces a buyer to purchase an item, even at a monopolistic price. If a seller offers a product for too high a price, buyers will refuse to purchase it, and then (it is hoped) the self-correcting action of Adam Smith's invisible hand will intervene and the seller either lower his price or new firms enter the market—all in the long run, of course. And while there is some truth in this account of the operation of market forces, and while, under the rare and elusive condition of "perfect competition" the market price can sometimes even be an indication of the just price, it is merely an indication. Market forces are not the reason for a just price, even when they may coincide with such a price. But in a capitalist economy, an economy characterized by the separation of ownership and work, many other factors must exist before we can begin to look at the market price as the just price. Although the concept of "marginal cost" is of little use in the real world, still the idea that the price should reflect a firm's costs gets at the heart of a calculation of a just price. Of course, cost includes a just wage for the producer, and Aquinas' statement in article four that we just noted, that the profit of a merchant should be simply a wage for his labor, reflects this understanding.

I have spoken of common estimation as a means of setting prices and just now I said "that the price should reflect a firm's costs gets at the heart of a calculation of a just price." Is there a contradiction here? No, for usually common estimation will implicitly take into account production costs. Pricing a new car at $59.95 violates our common estimation, certainly, but ultimately this is based on a recognition that such a price will cover only a fraction of the costs of producing a car. It is true that the more complex the process of manufacturing or the supply chain issues involved, the more likely it is that ordinary consumers might misjudge the cost of production. But the point still remains that generally our common estimation of a reasonable price will reflect roughly the cost of production of an item.

The next two articles both deal with defects in products and the seller's duty to make these known to potential buyers. Here again we meet with a point of radical difference from capitalism. Not only is it generally held today to be stupid to reveal an unseen defect, but firms spend large sums on advertising and promoting products that are defective or harmful. Indeed, this raises the entire issue of advertising. Speaking summarily, it seems hard to justify advertising that goes beyond informing consumers of the availability of products, information on new products, and so on. To entice people to buy what they do not need, either by exaggerating the good points of a product or, as seems more common, by creating some sort of image in the consumer's mind which connects the product with worldly success or romantic attraction would seem to be plainly wrong and impossible to justify.

Thomas' fourth article gets to the heart of commercial life by asking whether it is licit for someone by engaging in business (*negotiando*) to sell something at a higher price than he bought it for, i.e., to do this as an occupation. He sets forth definite criteria for any increase in selling price over purchase price. If the seller has made improvements in the product, if on account of a change of place or time the price has legitimately risen, if he underwent risk in exporting it somewhere - all these justify selling something for more than one paid for it. But clearly there is no justification here for unlimited profits. Every increase in cost must be accounted for by some definite title. So although one may licitly engage in commerce, the gain should be payment for one's labor or skill or risk.

We should also note the general attitude of St. Thomas toward commercial activity. Buying and selling which is for the sake of gain "is justly blamed (*juste vituperatur*) because it serves the desire for gain which knows no limit but tends into infinity. And therefore business (*negotiatio*) considered in itself has a certain baseness (*quamdam turpitudinem*) in so far as it does not imply of itself an honest or necessary end." St. Thomas is here not condemning economic activity, but economic activity removed from its natural end of serving mankind's natural needs. Adam and Eve were placed in the garden to tend it and eat of its fruit, not to start a business exporting produce. Although a certain amount of trade is certainly necessary, the further our economic activity is from fulfilling its natural and necessary purposes the greater the likelihood of the kinds of social and economic dislocations and disruptions that disfigure an economy and divert it from its primary end. It may seem like a hopelessly utopian ideal to undo the complex system of trade which we have developed, and certainly it is hardly something that can be implemented everywhere immediately. But it is one that we should constantly keep in mind as our goal. To buy at a farmers' market is to eliminate the middleman and approach this ideal. The fact that farmers' markets are a quaint exception in an otherwise corporate economy simply shows how far we have strayed from Aquinas' conception of healthy economic life. If we feel ourselves unable to embrace St. Thomas' standards, let us at least understand them and recognize their wisdom, and, perhaps, take what small steps we can toward actually attaining them.

6

Profit

Long about 1964, a Republican governor of Ohio
came out with the slogan, "Profit is not a dirty
word in Ohio." And many supporters of free-
market economics would no doubt like to shout out,
"Profit is not a dirty word, period." But dirty or not, I
suggest that profit is not a well-understood word or
idea. Let us examine how profit may be understood
and then see what the implications of that are for our
discussion of economics.

First what do we mean by the term? This is how
Msgr. John A. Ryan describes profit:

> [An entrepreneur] realizes that, after paying for labor
> of all sorts, returning interest to the capitalist and
> rent to the landowner, defraying the cost of repairs,
> and setting aside a fund to cover depreciation,
> [what] he has left for himself ... constitutes the
> share called profits.... [1]

Or in Paul Samuelson's definition, profit is "net rev-
enues, or the difference between total sales and total
costs." [2] This would seem a straightforward notion, and
in a sense it is. But what exactly does this sum mean?
Why is, or why should there be, something left over
for the businessman after all the expenses noted have
been paid? What elements enter into or justify this?

---

[1] John A. Ryan, *Distributive Justice* (New York: Macmillan, 3rd
ed., 1942), p. 176.
[2] *Microeconomics*, p. 27. Samuelson later (p. 274) distinguishes
business from *economic* profits. From the latter must be subtracted
"implicit or opportunity costs," including the unpaid labor of a
sole proprietor or "unpaid management time" which must be
compared against what these persons could have earned elsewhere,
i.e., against their opportunity cost of working where they did.

Should there be any limits to it? Msgr. Ryan, in the same paragraph of his that I just quoted, gives a clear answer to our questions. Profit, as he means it, is "the return for his [the entrepreneur's] labor of organization and direction, and for the risk that he underwent."

With this Msgr. Ryan gives an explicit reason and an implicit justification for profit. Profit comes from a twofold source. On the one hand, the business owner's "labor of organization and direction," on the other hand "the risk that he underwent." Now the first of these is actually a wage or salary for the owner, something to which he is surely entitled. Whether he has others working for him or not, the entrepreneur is almost always performing some sort of work of management, and possibly much more, for which he, like all other workers, deserves remuneration. The second title to profits, the risk that the businessman undergoes, is more complicated, and is peculiarly associated with a capitalist economy where business failures are common.

Risk can be for two reasons. One is the ordinary risk that any businessman undergoes. The second is the special type or degree of risk associated with a new or better product or service. In a capitalist economy there is always considerable risk, since the failure rate among businesses is high.[3] But in the case of a new product, there are extra expenses for making the public aware of it and its advantages, and so on. It seems fitting that someone who does take a risk to provide something

---

[3] According to Bureau of Labor Statistics data beginning in 1994, after five years nearly half of new business establishments had gone out of business and after ten years, about 65% (Entrepreneurship and the U. S. Economy," www.bls.gov/bdm/ entrepreneurship. htm). More recent data shows that only "34.7 percent of business establishments born in 2013 were still operating in 2023" (www. bls.gov/opub/ted/2024/34-7-percent-of-business-establishments-born-in-2013-were-still-operating-in-2023.html). Of course, some of these closures are mergers, purchases by other firms, etc. They are not all instances of bankruptcy.

new — provided of course that we are talking about a truly useful product — is entitled to some reward for that. In the case of ordinary risk involved in the operation of a business under capitalist conditions, it seems less clear that a special reward is due simply for that, for this is common to all or most business owners.

When profit, instead of being understood as recompense for labor and (possibly) reward for risk, is understood in Samuelson's terms *merely* as "the difference between total sales and total costs," there is no suggestion as to *why* such a sum should exist. It simply happens, and, naturally, those who enjoy the use of such profits would like them to be as large as possible. In this view there is no moral linkage between profits and the work or the risk of the owner — no moral linkage to anything. Thus if owners can manage to obtain huge profits that creates no moral problem, for profit (in this understanding) has and needs no moral justification. But when profit is specified in the manner that Msgr. Ryan does, as compensation for labor and risk, then we do have the suggestion that such profits must bear some reasonable relation to that labor and risk. For example, if someone taking a risk to provide a needed good or service is entitled to a reward, then presumably the greater the risk, the greater ought to be the reward. And if part of the profits received is compensation for the labor of the proprietor, similarly this should be in proportion to the amount and type of labor. If we accept Msgr. Ryan's understanding of what profits are, then the entrepreneur is not entitled to open-ended compensation, to whatever might happen to be "the difference between total sales and total costs," but his profits must bear some sort of reasonable relation to his work and risk. If a businessman is becoming immensely rich, especially in a short period of time, then there is reason to suspect that something is amiss: either his customers are being charged too much or he is not paying just wages to his workers.[4]

In a capitalist economy profit is rightly understood as comprising both wages for the entrepreneur or owner and some reasonable reward for risk. But most of the time the latter would not be a factor in a distributist economy. Why is this? In that type of economy reward for innovation or invention could well be handled in a formalized way by one's guild. That is, any discovery, say of a new method of production or an improved product, would automatically become the property of the guild as a whole, and its discoverer or inventor receive a reward from the guild. Moreover, we must remember that a guild economy tries to keep a rough balance between the public's need for a certain good or service and the provision of that service, so as to eliminate competition between producers, which leads to all the problems typical of a capitalist system. Therefore business failures would be much rarer and not simply a by-product of competitive conditions.

Samuelson makes no attempt to analyze the concept of profit. He simply notes that it exists. But when we do make such an attempt, we see the varying elements that constitute it. Only when we do that can we subject it to any moral judgment and recognize its place in the structure and functioning of a well-ordered economy.

---

[4] On this latter point, Pius XI clearly taught in *Quadragesimo Anno* that capitalists often claimed a larger share of the total economic product than they had a right to. "Capital . . . claimed all the . . . profits and left to the laborer the barest minimum . . . " (no. 54). "Every effort, therefore, must be made that at least in future only a fair share of the fruits of production be permitted to accumulate in the hands of the wealthy, and that an ample sufficiency be supplied to the workingmen" (no. 61).

7

Wages

In the past the question of wages and wage justice was not as important to mankind as it is today in our capitalist economy, precisely because under capitalism, that is, the separation of ownership and work, the greatest number of people will in fact work for wages. Hence today questions concerning wage justice will frequently arise. Wages exist because the relation of employer and employee exists. Although the Church, as expressed in the statement of Pope Leo XIII in *Rerum Novarum*, no. 46, that, "The law, therefore, should favor ownership, and its policy should be to induce as many people as possible to become owners," desires to minimize the extent of the employer/employee relationship by making workers owners and owners workers, this is far from the practice today, and in any social order, however ideal, some aspects of the wage relationship will certainly continue to exist. And although beginning at least with Leo XIII the popes have again and again reiterated the teaching that "the wage paid to the workingman should be sufficient for the support of himself and of his family" (Pius XI, *Quadragesimo Anno*, no. 71), many, even among those who consider themselves to be obedient and faithful Catholics, are not entirely comfortable with this repeated teaching, despite the fact that probably it can by now be said to be an infallible teaching by virtue of the ordinary magisterium.[1] To a great extent this

---

[1] For the repetition of this teaching, see *inter alia*, Leo XIII, *Rerum Novarum* nos. 43–45; Pius XI, *Casti Connubii*, no. 117, *Quadragesimo Anno*, nos. 71, 110, *Divini Redemptoris*, no. 49; John XXIII, *Mater et Magistra*, no. 71; John Paul II, *Centesimus Annus*, no. 8.

discomfort can be attributed to the understanding of economics that sees the economy as basically a self-regulating machine, with wages determined more or less automatically by the interaction of certain variables, and therefore to interject ethical constraints into this mechanism, contrary to the mechanical interplay of economic forces, endangers the successful working of the entire economy. Additionally, such Catholics are often under the impression that any attempt to inter-vene in the economy is necessarily socialistic, and thus (as they suppose) contrary to the Church's teaching.

Those who think in this manner will argue that in the case of certain jobs, e.g., a worker in a fast food restaurant or a janitor or a farm worker, the variables of labor supply and demand determine a wage which in fact is usually below a living family wage, but that this is simply a fact of economic life. If we attempt to tamper with it, we risk unraveling the entire structure of our economy.

The very title of Samuelson's chapter, "How Markets Determine Incomes," indicates clearly the mechanical approach to wages and income distribution, which is simply

> a special case of the theory of prices. Wages are really only the price of labor; rents are similarly the price for using land. Moreover, the prices of factors of production are primarily set by the interaction between supply and demand for different factors — just as the prices of goods are largely determined by the supply and demand for goods.[2]

Thus the different incomes of different kinds of workers can be explained by means of a typical demand curve. Since "the supply of surgeons is severely limited [and] [d]emand for surgery is growing rapidly... surgeons earn \$270,000 a year on average." On the other hand,

---

[2] *Microeconomics*, p. 229.

"fast-food . . . jobs have no skill or educational require-
ments and are open to virtually everyone. The supply
is highly elastic.... Wages are close to the minimum
wage because of the ease of entry into this market,
and the average full-time employee makes $12,000 a
year."[3] To many people this type of reasoning seems
so obvious that one can understand their difficulties
with the papal teaching on wage justice cited earlier.
Within the framework of neoclassical economics it
does indeed seem obvious.

There are many things one can say against such a
deficient understanding of how wages should be determined. In the first place, we may look at the common-
sense teaching of Pope Leo XIII in *Rerum Novarum*.
Leo noted that

> a man's labor has two notes or characters. First of
> all, it is *personal*; for the exertion of individual power
> belongs to the individual who puts it forth, employ-
> ing this power for that personal profit for which
> it was given. Secondly, a man's labor is *necessary*;
> for without the results of labor a man cannot live;
> and self-conservation is a law of nature, which it is
> wrong to disobey. Now, if we were to consider labor
> merely so far as it is *personal*, doubtless it would
> be within the workman's right to accept any rate
> of wages whatever; for in the same way as he is
> free to work or not, so he is free to accept a small
> remuneration or even none at all. But this is a mere
> abstract supposition; the labor of the working man
> is not only his personal attribute, but it is *necessary*;
> and this makes all the difference. The preservation
> of life is the bounden duty of each and all, and to
> fail therein is a crime. It follows that each one has
> a right to procure what is required in order to live;
> and the poor can procure it in no other way than
> by work and wages. (no. 44)

---

[3] *Microeconomics*, p. 236.

In other words, if mankind must work to procure what is necessary for life, and this is a duty imposed generally upon all of us, then how can one fulfill that duty unless he receives a just wage, that is, a wage "sufficient to maintain himself, his wife, and his children in reasonable comfort" (*Rerum Novarum*, no. 46)? Hence,

> there is a dictate of nature more imperious and more ancient than any bargain between man and man, that the remuneration must be enough to support the wage-earner in reasonable and frugal comfort. If through necessity or fear of a worse evil, the workman accepts harder conditions because an employer or contractor will give him no better, he is the victim of force and injustice. (no. 45)

Without such a wage a worker is reduced to the inhuman toil of working sixteen or eighteen hours a day, or compelling wife and children to work for wages outside the home. This would be to institute something little better than slavery for the majority of the human race.

There is another very interesting and creative way to approach the question of wage justice, however, that of the just wage as the "economically correct wage," a concept elaborated by Heinrich Pesch. His argument ultimately rests upon a different understanding of both economics and economies, and the contrast in his approach with the approach of neoclassical and related schools can help one to see that the latter is not the only reasonable way of understanding economic phenomena, and in fact that Pesch's approach is consonant with the Catholic understanding of man, society and the state, as well as actual economic facts.

Pesch, a German Jesuit priest who lived from 1854 to 1926, studied economics at the University of Berlin, and wrote several scholarly, multi-volume works on economics and economic philosophy. His most famous work is the *Lehrbuch der Nationalökonomie*, which appeared in five volumes in German between 1905 and

1923, and which comprises ten volumes in its English translation.[4] Pesch was more than an economist and a commentator on papal teaching, for in a sense he helped shape the direction of papal social doctrine itself, since his thought provided the background for Pius XI and his advisors when they drafted the 1931 encyclical *Quadragesimo Anno*. Furthermore his influence is very evident in the social thought of John Paul II. Pesch, in fact, coined the term solidarism or solidarity so extensively used by that pontiff.

Pesch's discussion of the just wage is largely contained in the second part of volume V of his *Lehrbuch*, and is one of his most original and interesting contributions to economic and moral theory, for he treats of the just wage as "the economically correct wage." As is usual for Pesch, he first grounds his economic thought in a philosophic understanding of man and human life, and he begins his discussion of wages in this way. "*The capacity to work* is a *natural good* of man, which is destined and therefore also empowered by nature, or by the Author of nature, to provide the worker with his necessary sustenance."[5]

If we believe that even after man's fall into sin the providence and goodness of God continue to rule his creation, then we recognize a definite harmony still existing in the world. The fact that God has given mankind the capacity and means to work indicates that he intends work as the means of supplying our necessities. But one man has only so many hours, so much physical or mental strength, to apply to work. Moreover, there is more to human life than mere survival, including

---

[4] *Lehrbuch der Nationalökonomie/Teaching Guide to Economics*, translated by Rupert Ederer, (Lewiston, N.Y.: Edwin Mellen Press, 2003). Ederer also translated and edited a one volume abridgement of Pesch's *Lehrbuch*, entitled *Heinrich Pesch on Solidarist Economics: Excerpts from the Lehrbuch der Nationalökonomie*, (Lanham, Maryland: University Press of America, c. 1998).

[5] *Lehrbuch*, vol. V, book, 2, p. 86. Emphasis in original throughout.

marriage and the family, and the creation, preservation and enjoyment of the human cultural patrimony. Thus it is not reasonable to expect someone to work eighteen hours a day, and if most people did that, the human race itself would perish or descend into a semi-human barbarism.

However, in fact it is rarely necessary for people to work eighteen hours in order to survive. Man's labor does not "have only the *natural destiny* to acquire for the worker his subsistence.... It also has the *natural capacity* to do so," Pesch continues.[6] In other words a normal adult person, working a reasonable number of hours a day, will generally be able to produce enough of economic value to provide not only for himself but for a family as well, provided of course that he has the tools, raw material and other necessities for whatever kind of work he does, as well as the personal habits and training required.

This relationship is exhibited most clearly in an economy consisting as much as is reasonably possible of owner-workers. But even in an economy characterized by the separation of ownership and work, an economy in which the wage is the usual means of personal and familial sustenance, this natural relation between our needs and our capacity to supply them should hold good. If it does not hold good, then something is wrong. Either someone is exploiting the worker by taking some of the economic value due to him, or the worker does not have enough capital (tools, land, machines) for his work to produce its naturally intended effect. This latter could even happen with a worker-owner if he did not have adequate tools or machines or if he possessed substandard or insufficient land.

If this is the case, let us look further at Fr. Pesch's approach and how he undercuts the presuppositions of

---

[6] *Lehrbuch*, vol. V, book, 2, p. 90.

the neoclassical understanding of wage determination. "The human ability to work retains the natural capacity to provide a livelihood even when it does not succeed in doing so actually," he begins. And he goes on to look at some examples of this type of situation which might arise in a capitalist economy.

> The employer who, by his own ineptitude, uses labor in such a way that it does not come up to doing what it is capable of doing, would nevertheless be required to pay the kind of wage which labor is intended to provide. However, if labor is utilized properly in accordance with its natural purpose, and the employer pays a wage which does not provide for labor's livelihood, then he violates *commutative justice*. Finally, an industry which, even under normal circumstances is not in a position to pay wages corresponding to what wages are supposed to accomplish, is *lacking in economic justification*. This means that the requisite consumer demand is lacking, and such an industry no longer has a place in the pattern of satisfying normal human wants.[7]

Let us look at this more carefully to see its significance. Pesch considers three separate cases here. In the first place, suppose someone employed a perfectly healthy worker but from neglect gave him only inferior tools, faulty material, broken machinery to work with, and then complained that he could not produce enough each day to pay him an adequate wage. This is the "employer who, by his own ineptitude, uses labor in such a way that it does not come up to doing what it is capable of doing." Such an employer, however, is nevertheless "required to pay the kind of wage which labor is intended to provide," for it is the employer's fault that the worker cannot create the economic value which his work is destined for and which he is perfectly capable of producing.

---

[7] *Lehrbuch*, vol. V, book, 2, p. 90.

Secondly, we have the case where "labor is utilized properly in accordance with its natural purpose, [but] the employer pays a wage which does not provide for labor's livelihood," which is a clear case of the violation of commutative justice.

Finally, we have the most interesting case of all, "an industry which, even under normal circumstances is not in a position to pay wages corresponding to what wages are supposed to accomplish. . . . " This industry is therefore "lacking in economic justification," which "means that the requisite consumer demand is lacking, and such an industry no longer has a place in the pattern of satisfying normal human wants." In this third scenario, we have the case in which the only way in which an employer can afford to sell his product is to make his prices so low that he cannot afford to pay his workers a living wage. Clearly then his product lacks sufficient consumer demand. It is as if he had to bribe the public to buy his products by charging less than their genuine production cost. The products are desired only because they are cheap. Today we are inundated with cheap goods produced abroad, sometimes in conditions little better than slavery. This is a distortion of the economic process as well as a violation of justice. If the good is worth buying, it is worth paying a price that fully compensates all who are involved in its production, including certainly workers. If someone revived legal slavery today and boasted that he could undersell his competitors because his labor costs were so low, who would doubt but that his entire enterprise was an economic as well as a moral evil, no matter how cheaply he could produce and sell his product? Or if a certain chain store sold only stolen goods and thus could largely eliminate its wholesale buying expenses, would not this constitute a violation of both justice and sound economics? The same logic must be applied to any enterprise which cannot afford to pay its workers a just wage. In all these cases employers are cheating, they are seeking to avoid their full production costs. This has no place in a normal economy in which labor fulfills its intrinsic purpose of providing for human life and in which work, production, buying and selling, all cooperate toward a situation in which human persons live and work together in justice and prosperity.

If I am willing to buy certain goods only if they are produced with the advantage of low-wage labor then I effectively proclaim that such goods do not belong within a normal economic system. If I am willing to patronize certain stores or restaurants only because their labor costs are so low, what does that say about my real demand for their products? I want it only if its price is below what is necessary for the cycle of exchange to be effective. For if everyone were paid substandard wages, or if the goods of honest suppliers were regularly stolen and sold at discounts, there would eventually be no buying and selling. An economy can function only so long as there is a market for the goods and services produced, which occurs only when labor receives a share of the national income sufficient to pay for those goods and services. Now we have the situation where in fact the exchange economy is subsidized by workers in industries who themselves do not earn enough to be genuine participants in real, human economic exchange. We have an economy that depends, and thinks it must depend, on what amounts to quasi-slave labor or substandard wage labor, labor that is not reimbursed sufficiently so that it can take its own part in the cycle of buying and selling.

Any owner, in addition to the staff which he hires, depends on other people or firms to keep his businesses running, on those who supply raw materials, who provide electricity, and so on. Would he object to paying those who provide raw materials or electricity what they need to keep their businesses running and even make a profit? Does mainstream economics begrudge a fair return on their economic input to anyone other than workers? Why are workers alone supposed to make an economic contribution without necessarily receiving a sufficient return? Any owner knows that his suppliers cannot decrease the prices they charge below a certain minimum because otherwise they could not stay in business. But apparently the case of workers is different, and if they can make no more than $12,000 a year that is nobody's fault, just the inexorable working of economic laws.

In recent decades income inequality has increased in the United States, with the share of aggregate income received by the economically lowest 20% of households declining from 4.0 in 1967 to 3.0 in 2022, while the share of income received by the top 20% increased from 43.6 to 52.1 in the same period, and the top 5% of households went from 17.2 to 23.5.[8] One way that families have been able to survive economically during this time is by having both parents work. Yet what does this create? Children raised without proper supervision, increased family and marital stress, even an increased demand for cheap food outside the home because of a lack of time to make good food at home. One moral and economic evil spawns many others, as is always the case in human affairs. We cannot expect to exploit labor and have a healthy, well-functioning society.

To recapitulate, if we look at the working capacity of a normal human being, we see both his inherent tendency and real ability to provide an adequate living for himself and his family, provided that he has sufficient capital goods to work with. In a simple owner-worker operation, this is evident. An economy consisting of

---

[8] Table H-2. Share of Aggregate Income Received by Each Fifth and Top 5 Percent of All Households: 1967 to 2022. www.census. gov/data/tables/time-series/demo/income-poverty /historical-income-inequality.html

such owner-workers would be characterized by a cycle of exchange in which producers received economic equivalents for the goods they produced by means of their work and which they exchanged for goods produced and sold likewise by their neighbors. The cycle of exchange would allow each producer to obtain "sufficient for the support of himself and of his family."

With capitalism, that is, the separation of owner-ship and work, complexities necessarily arise. But even in such a relationship this tendency and capacity of human work to provide for human needs continues. Heinrich Pesch presents three possibilities of failure on the part of capitalists to pay a just wage. In the third case we have an example of an entire industry or subset of an industry which does not fit into the cycle of exchange which characterizes a normal and healthy economy. Pesch shows that if we look at the purpose of human work and of the economy we see that our economic activity obviously must provide a living for those who participate in it. The understanding of economics typified by Paul Samuelson signally fails to do this, while Heinrich Pesch provides an alternative way of looking at an economy consistent both with Catholic teaching and with a correct understanding of the purpose of human work.

8
Unemployment

The thesis of this chapter is that unemployment is a pseudo-problem. By calling it that, I do not mean that unemployment does not exist, or that it is not a very serious concern for the unemployed, their families and for society as a whole. What I mean and will argue here is that unemployment is not something natural to economic life, but is a problem created almost entirely by the complexities of our economy, and which is taken for granted by the academic discipline of economics only because that discipline has long been captive to the ideology of capitalism.

The study of economics developed as a theoretical elaboration of capitalism and industrialism as they began to come to maturity in Europe in the 18th century and afterwards. Most often mainstream economic thought has not only assumed capitalism, but has been a mouthpiece for capitalism, in fact, a sophisticated attempt to provide a justification for the disparity in incomes and for the social dislocations that are such notable characteristics of the capitalist world. In face of this complex structure of thought, it can be helpful to return to the basics of human behavior upon which economic life is based in order to discover a different and more accurate way of conceptualizing mankind's economic activity.

Let us first look at the three different types of economic unemployment as these are enumerated and acknowledged by economists.[1] First, and of little

---

[1] Note that I am dealing with unemployment as an *economic* question only. It is arguable that there exists what might be called *cultural* unemployment, but this is outside of the scope of this book.

importance for our discussion, there is voluntary or otherwise short-term unemployment of people between jobs, between school and a job, and so on. This is sometimes referred to by economists as *frictional* unemployment. If the other two types of unemployment are eliminated or reduced, this type will be of little concern.

> Then there is what economists call *structural* unemployment, which Paul Samuelson describes as a mismatch between the supply of and the demand for workers. Mismatches can occur because the demand for one kind of labor is rising while the demand for another kind is falling, and supplies do not quickly adjust.... [For example], the demand for coal miners has been depressed for decades because of the lack of geographical mobility of labor and capital: unemployment rates in coal-mining communities remain high today.[2]

Thirdly, there is *cyclical* unemployment, which Samuelson explains as occurring "when the overall demand for labor is low. As total spending and output fall, unemployment rises virtually everywhere."[3]

These latter two types of unemployment require separate discussion. First let us look at the question of structural unemployment. It arises chiefly because of new technology or on account of some external cause, such as, in the case of coal miners, heightened concerns about air pollution. The former cause, new technology, is the more common occurrence. In an economy dominated by those who own the means of production, new technology presents an opportunity for higher profits achieved via lower costs. A new or improved device usually makes a certain number of workers unnecessary. Since labor is a cost item in a firm's balance sheet, there is rarely any conflict in

---

[2] *Macroeconomics*, p. 259.
[3] *Macroeconomics*, p. 259.

the capitalist's mind about what to do: if he can save money by eliminating workers and buying machines he will do so. But if workers themselves controlled the enterprises in which they worked, either individually or cooperatively, there would be other considerations besides merely increased profits. New technology can and will be adopted, but the timing and rate of its adoption would be balanced against other equally important economic and social needs, such as job and family security, social stability, and the like.

Moreover, we should recognize that technology can develop in more than one way, and that replacing workers by machines is not the only way to secure improved production. In any case, if we remember that the economy is an important but subordinate part of human social life, we will not regard technological improvements as the *summum bonum*. Right now, with capitalists mostly calling the shots in the economy, their view usually prevails, and what we call economic efficiency wins against any of the human concerns and needs that an economy is supposedly subservient to. If an economy could do without workers altogether and produce more cheaply and quickly solely by means of robots, would this really be a benefit to mankind? Would not the fact that the now unemployed workers could no longer afford to buy any of the robot-produced goods signify that such an economy had entirely inverted means and ends?

What if technological advances across the board make it possible for our consumption needs to be supplied by merely a portion of the labor force? The obvious answer to that is, if it is no longer necessary for everyone to work eight hours to supply mankind's needs, let everyone work a little or a lot less, simply enough so that mankind's needs are taken care of. If this can be done with everyone working six hours instead of eight, well and good. Here, though, we run into one of the shibboleths of neoclassical economics, the so-called "lump of labor fallacy." Paul Samuelson explains this notion as follows:

> Whenever unemployment is high, people often think that the solution lies in spreading existing work more evenly among the labor force. For example, Europe in the 1990s suffered extremely high unemployment, and many labor leaders and politicians suggested that the solution was to reduce the workweek so that the same number of hours would be worked by all the workers. This view—that the amount of work to be done is fixed—is called the lump of labor fallacy.

What is wrong with this idea, according to Samuelson?

> [T]he lump of labor argument implies that there is only so much remunerative work to be done.... A careful examination of economic history... shows that an increase in labor supply can be accommodated by higher employment, although that increase may require lower real wages.[4]

What is one to make of this argument? If we examine it, Samuelson appears to mean that if workers are willing to work for lower wages, some capitalist will employ them to produce something that he thinks he can sell, and thus absorb the unemployed workers. This is no doubt often true, but this says nothing about the relationship between the total amount of goods being produced at a certain point in time, the total number of workers or potential workers existing at that time, and how that work is to be apportioned among them. At the point when the unemployment in question arises, why is it not a reasonable policy to distribute the work more evenly? If the economy hitherto has been producing a sufficient amount of goods to supply consumption needs, and then unemployment increases due to

---

[4] *Microeconomics*, pp. 257–58.

technological changes and consequently a reduced need for human labor, clearly the total quantity of potential workforce effort is now greater than is needed. Thus reducing everyone's hours seems like an entirely reasonable response. Society possesses the productive capacity to satisfy consumer needs but no longer requires the same amount of labor. Thus both the amount of work, as well as the product of work, can be redistributed among the total labor force, taking into account the new technology.

The fact that Samuelson thinks that only by employing workers at lowered wages can this problem be addressed shows that he is assuming as a fact of nature the position of dominance by capitalists and the corresponding subordinate position of workers. Of course, capitalists are not likely to pay workers the same wage they previously received if they now work fewer hours. But both the productive capacities of the workers remain the same, society's need for goods and services remains the same (in the short run), while the economy's capacity to produce has increased. Any mismatch is in the nexus between the worker and the means of production. A response that has regard both for the purpose of an economy and its connection with the social fabric as a whole would see reduced work hours as a logical response to the situation.

Next let us look at the question of cyclical unemployment, that type which comes about "when the overall demand for labor is low" because of a business cycle downturn. Business cycles are those alternating periods of boom and bust which are the causes for the cyclical decrease in the demand for labor, and which come about because of capitalism's propensity toward overproduction and speculation. "A business cycle is a swing in total national output, income, and employment, usually lasting for a period of 2 to 10 years, marked by widespread expansion or contraction in most sectors of the economy."[5] Although everyone living in a capitalist economy is familiar with such cycles, or their effects, one might wonder why, apart from special and external factors such as famines, natural disasters, wars, migrations, and so on, such cycles exist. Consumer demand for necessary and reasonable goods normally will not fluctuate much—demand for food, clothing, housing, books and the like. Nor will the size of the workforce, and hence the economy's ability to produce goods, usually experience sudden short-term major decreases or increases. Thus there is no reason to expect the two most important factors in an economy, demand and the ability to supply that demand, to change significantly in a short period of time. Of course, the external factors I mentioned can cause a sudden and large increase or decrease in either demand or the capacity to supply that demand. They are simply an inescapable part of life on this earth. But there are factors which are peculiar to capitalism which have caused probably the majority of business cycles, at least the majority of those which have occurred in recent decades.

The tendency in capitalism is simply production for the sake of sales, not production for the sake of reasonable use. Thus the tendency to overproduce is always present because the capitalist class, people one step or more removed from actual production, have little or no interest in production for use as such. Capitalism is fueled by an imperative of production for the sake of sales, regardless of consumers' needs or of their spontaneous desires for the goods or services in question. As such, it always rests upon foundations which are liable to be shaken. But such demand, which is usually artificially stimulated by advertising, is necessarily fickle or fragile. The artificial desire for larger or more

---

[5] *Macroeconomics*, p. 125.

luxurious houses or cars, for example, tends to drive up prices of those goods, and can lead to so-called *bubbles* in which prices rise exponentially. Eventually these bubbles will burst and prices will decline, sometimes considerably. Such extreme up and down movements of prices can cause numerous related economic dislocations, such as panics or depressions, which are simply instances of severe business cycles. "History is marked by bubbles in which speculative prices were driven up far beyond their intrinsic value.... Speculative bubbles always produce crashes and sometimes lead to economic panics."[6]

But if we consider the fundamentals of economic activity, we will see that God created human beings with both the capacity for work and the need to consume. In fact, these two characteristics balance one another in that wherever there are people, there are both producers and consumers. Thus it would seem that everywhere people can do the work which supplies them with the goods they need. The human capacity for work corresponds roughly with our need for the products of that work. The more people, the more workers, the fewer people, the fewer workers. What does this have to do with the question of unemployment? If in general each person is able to perform productive work sufficient to supply at least his own needs, then why should anyone be idled, unable to work? Does not each person create his own demand and at the same time provide the means for supplying that demand?

The reason that any particular person's capacity for work cannot be the means for supplying his needs is usually because he is denied access to the means of production, to land or tools, for example. On occasion a harsh environment makes it difficult to take

---

[6] *Macroeconomics*, p. 177.

advantage of mankind's capacity to produce, but this is not the usual case. This is not a problem, then, that arises from the nature of economic activity, it is an organizational problem, one ultimately occasioned by the question of who owns or controls land or tools. The more complicated the relationship between individuals and the means of production, the more likely will be some sort of organizational or structural difficulty which impedes people's ability to work and produce. Capitalism heightens this tendency not only by the complexity of its structure, but by creating a class of owners whose primary and direct interest is not in producing for the needs of mankind, but in convincing people to buy their product, whether needed or not, whether well-made or not.

We can see how the complexity of a capitalist structuring of the economy contributes to the imbalances that create cyclical unemployment if we contrast that with a very simple distributist model of an economy. In such an economy, one in which all workers owned their land and tools and produced whatever was needed for themselves and their families, the immediate connection between work and consumption would be obvious, since each person would be the primary producer of most or all of what he and his family needed, and the one-to-one correspondence between a worker's need to consume and his ability to produce would be obvious. Of course such an economy is hardly possible outside of a primitive level of culture, and in any case is not desirable. The division of labor, though it can be extended too far, has obvious benefits to humanity. Indeed, the medieval urban economy of guilds assumed and fostered the division of labor up to a point. But what we should note here is that the more complex the connection or relationship between workers and the means of production, the more possibility that a worker will be hindered in the exercise of his ability to produce. Distributism tries to keep that connection as simple as a reasonable division of labor and other necessary factors will allow, while capitalism needlessly elaborates that by shifting emphasis from production for fulfillment of human needs, to production oriented toward sales, toward new products that often have little utility, together with a constant preoccupation with higher profit margins, so that capital seeks not merely a sufficient return, but an ever higher one.

Any society and economy that is structured toward man's genuine welfare ought to seek to make use of the obvious connection between the human need to consume and the human ability to work and produce. This must be kept front and center in our economic thinking, and any needless elaborations and complexities which are introduced into the economy must be eliminated or at least watched carefully lest they create conditions, such as unemployment, which are socially or economically harmful.

In addition to the three types of economic unemployment that economists note, there is another type which they are reluctant to acknowledge, or at least to regard as a significant problem. This is unemployment caused by trade agreements. Although the trade facilitated by agreements such as NAFTA can be called free only with numerous qualifications, still it is usually in the direction of freer trade that such agreements lead. Such trade pacts are based on the neoclassical doctrine of comparative advantage, which Paul Samuelson calls "one of the deepest truths in all of economics."[7]

Comparative advantage is based upon a fact, to be sure, that different countries excel better at some products than others, and from this it is argued that it is in the interests of all countries to specialize in

---

[7] *Macroeconomics*, p. 388.

the products that they can produce most efficiently in order to increase the overall material living standard of all countries. While superficially plausible, in fact there are major objections against the theory. In the first place, it treats each country as if it were merely a site for production, ignoring cultural or legal factors. For example, the unique cultural and legal situation of Mexico included Indian villages which held land in common and which in consequence were able to be self-supporting in food. Trade agreements which require land to be freely bought and sold destroy such communities, despite any elegant graphs that economists concoct purporting to prove that everyone will be better off under these agreements. More fundamentally, the theory of comparative advantage assumes that more and more stuff, what is called economic growth, is the *summum bonum* of human life. Consider Samuelson's discussion of objections to international trade agreements.

> But this does not mean that every individual, firm, sector, or factor of production will benefit from trade.... Recent studies indicate that unskilled workers in high-income countries have suffered reductions in real wages in the last three decades because of the increased imports of goods from low-wage developing countries....
> The theory of comparative advantage shows that other sectors will gain more than the injured sectors will lose. Moreover, over long periods of time, those displaced from low-wage sectors eventually gravitate to higher-wage jobs.... Nations that disregard comparative advantage pay a heavy price in terms of their living standards and economic growth.[8]

Unfortunately, "over long periods of time" most of those unskilled workers will be dead long before they

---

[8] *Microeconomics*, p. 306.

manage to "gravitate to higher-wage jobs," and in the meantime the towns and cities in which they live will be devastated, their families often hurt, social problems will increase, and in general the real standard of living—which is not measured in terms of how much stuff we possess—will decline. The overall amount of available commodities might increase, at least for some people, such as economics professors, but at the cost of buying goods produced by poorly-treated workers in "low-wage developing countries." International trade *can* be beneficial to all parties, but only if many more factors besides the total quantity of goods produced and sold are considered. An awareness of the purpose of both human life as a whole, and of economic activity as a subordinate part of life, would motivate us to create a society which did not give material goods a greater value than they deserve. As St. John Paul II wrote in his encyclical *Centesimus Annus,*

> It is not wrong to want to live better; what is wrong is a style of life which is presumed to be better when it is directed toward "having" rather than "being," which wants to have more, not in order to be more but in order to spend life in enjoyment as an end in itself. (no. 36)

Mainstream economic thought is based on the idea that human life is not about "being," but about "having," about, as Samuelson avers, producing enough stuff so that "the average American could live at the level of the average doctor or big-league baseball player." This is nothing other than a philosophy concocted in Hell, a point of view opposed to any Christian conception of life. International trade need not create unemployment, but it will do so if it is based on the notion that any increase in the amount of commodities produced, sold or traded, is a good thing, regardless of any ill effect it has on human life, individual or social.

Unemployment need not exist, or at least, need not be the problem that it so often is in today's economy. If we are willing to rethink economic principles in the light of fundamentals, then we will see that there is a way out of the orientation of economic activity which has diverted it from its natural end of providing for the genuine consumption needs of mankind.

9

Property

Property in its various forms is among the most important of economic institutions. But our thinking about it is frequently confused and therefore results in erroneous conclusions. As I have mentioned over and over again in this book, usually the key to understanding something is via the concept of its *final cause*— that for the sake of which it exists or is done or operates. The basic purpose of something acts as a limit on it, in the sense that whenever our use of any process or thing disrupts the very purpose for which that process or thing is primarily intended, there is at least a potential moral problem present. This concept is one of the missing elements in most of modern thought, and has made many of our modern discussions of important issues pretty much pointless.

How does this apply to property? Well, just as our morality about food and sex must be in accord with their primary purposes, so it is with property. It too has a purpose, and as in the case of food and sex, it is not too difficult to discern what it is. It is for the orderly provision of the things we need for human life, for supporting one's family, for obtaining the goods upon which a truly human culture is based, in short, for all that is necessary for the common good of a society. The acquisition of external goods is not an end in itself, but is for the sake of our family life, our community life, our intellectual life, our spiritual life, or as Pope John Paul II put it in *Centesimus Annus*, as "necessary for one's personal development and the development of one's family" (no. 6).

Property has a purpose; therefore it has its proper limitations. This purpose is not something imposed upon it, but is inherent in any right conception of it. Thus limitations on property ownership in accordance with property's purpose are not an infringement on personal rights. If laws against polygamy are just, it is hard to see how laws regulating property are unjust. Both restrict only *dis*ordered human freedom.

It is our human nature that ultimately determines or suggests what is "necessary for one's personal development and the development of one's family." One person can only eat so much food or wear so many clothes. If I have fifty pairs of shoes, in all probability I will keep most of them in my closet and never or rarely wear them, because that number of shoes has no rational relationship to my need for shoes. If I own ten houses, probably I will spend very little time in most of them and so those houses will hardly serve the purpose for which houses exist. And so on. Our temporal needs are determined by the nature which God gave us, which should be the regulator of our acquisition and use of external goods. As St. Thomas wrote " . . . the appetite of natural riches is not infinite, because according to a set measure they satisfy nature; but the appetite of artificial riches [i.e., token wealth] is infinite, because it serves inordinate concupiscence. . . . "[1]

Catholic teaching on the subject of property is quite nuanced, recognizing the differing historical and cultural circumstances in which property exists and grounding its justification for property rights in the common good. Pius XI in his 1931 encyclical *Quadragesimo Anno* devotes sections 44–52 to a careful discussion of property, its rights and the limitations on those rights. He notes the historical fact that different ages and cultures have had differing understandings of this right.

> History proves that the right of ownership, like other
> elements of social life, is not absolutely rigid, and

---

[1] *Summa Theologiae*, I-II, q. 2, a. 1, ad 3.

this doctrine We Ourselves have given utterance to
on a previous occasion in the following terms: "How
varied are the forms which the right of property
has assumed! First, a primitive form in use among
untutored and backward peoples, which still exists
in certain localities even in our own day; then, that
of the patriarchal age; later came various tyrannical
types (We use the word in its classical meaning);
finally the feudal and monarchic systems down to
the varieties of more recent times." (no. 49)

The Pope continues that "the State has by no means
the right to abolish" private property, but it does have
the right "to control its use and bring it into harmony
with the interests of the public good." Thus

> when civil authority adjusts ownership to meet the
> needs of the public good it acts not as an enemy, but
> as the friend of private owners; for thus it effectively
> prevents the possession of private property, intended
> by Nature's Author in His Wisdom for the sustaining
> of human life, from creating intolerable burdens
> and so rushing to its own destruction. It does not
> therefore abolish, but protects private ownership,
> and far from weakening the right to private property,
> it gives it new strength. (no. 49)

In *Laborem Exercens* John Paul II spells this out more
explicitly,

> Christian tradition has never upheld this right [to
> property] as absolute and untouchable. On the
> contrary, it has always understood this right within
> the broader context of the right common to all to
> use the goods of the whole of creation: *the right to
> private property is subordinated to the right to common
> use*, to the fact that goods are meant for everyone.
> (no. 14)[2]

---

[2] Cf. *Centesimus Annus* (no. 6), where John Paul wrote that Leo
XIII in *Rerum Novarum* was "well aware that private property is
not an absolute value...."

Indeed, Paul VI, in *Populorum Progressio* (1967) goes as far as to state that when there exist "large and sometimes very extensive rural estates which are only slightly cultivated or not cultivated at all," it can be lawful to expropriate these estates in order to provide land for the poor, with compensation for the prior owners (no. 71). Thus we must judge the right to property not by Enlightenment notions of an absolute right to private property, but by a Catholic understanding of that right based upon the purpose for which property exists.

Different kinds of property have different moral justifications and hence different potential limitations. We may distinguish at least the following types of property:

- *Individual* or *family*, which can consist of a dwelling place or individual productive property (a small business or farm) or savings or investments of some kind above and beyond what is strictly necessary for reasonable and decent family life.

- *Corporate property*, that is, property owned by some entity possessed of legal personality. This could be a business corporation but equally a university or an association of some kind.

- *Private communal property*, which was often based on traditional or customary law, an uncommon form of property today, especially in the United States, but very common in the past and still existing in some places. For example, it might comprise common grazing land or bodies of water for fishing, but without formal ownership vested in any particular person or group.

- *State property*, often simply called public property, but to be distinguished from private communal property, which might equally be termed public property.

Since each of these forms of property has different purposes and different kinds or degrees of justification in relation to the common good, they each are subject to different limitations or restrictions. Let us examine each of these in more detail.

1) When we look at individual or family property we should be able to discern a difference between a home or a small business and savings or investments. This is not to say that savings and investments are wrong. But taxation of these different properties might vary quite a bit. Taxes on homes or small business, where they exist, ought to be moderate, while taxes on savings and investments could be taxed at a graduated scale which might rise sharply. The teaching of Paul VI in *Populorum Progressio* concerning the possible confiscation of "large and sometimes very extensive rural estates which are only slightly cultivated or not cultivated at all,"(no. 71) pertains to what is in effect investment property, not to a family home or a business or farm that provides family income. Again, the proposal, made by some writers, for the "conscription" in wartime not merely of men but of wealth would seem to apply properly to savings and investments rather than to homes or small productive property. The point is that the common good requires that individuals and families possess the kind and amount of property necessary or helpful to support their existence and well-being. Hence Leo XIII's statement in *Rerum Novarum* that "The law, therefore, should favor ownership, and its policy should be to induce as many people as possible to become owners" (no. 46). Savings and investments, while not in themselves wrong, and often even useful, are not as necessary as the former types of property and therefore have less of an absolute justification. But even here we can distinguish between savings, say, that provide support in old age and savings that represent what is really superfluous wealth. Since such superfluous wealth, like all property, possesses its justification in relation to the common good, it clearly must yield to the demands and needs of the society as a whole, especially in times of emergency.

One of the justifications that Pope Leo XIII advances in *Rerum Novarum* for the ownership of private property is that,

> Men always work harder and more readily when they
> work on that which is their own; nay, they learn to
> love the very soil which yields in response to the
> labor of their hands, not only food to eat, but an
> abundance of the good things for themselves and
> those that are dear to them. (no. 47)

Where property is conceived of as having a real connection with an individual or a family, an attitude prevails that naturally recognizes its purpose and likewise
the absurdity of excessive concentrations of property.
The dispute between our modern notion of property
and the classical Christian understanding, then, is not
fundamentally a dispute about the details of property
ownership, but about the very conception we have of
property, of society, and at bottom of man himself;
just as both Pius XI and John Paul II point out that the
root error of socialism is not economic, but an error
about the nature of man and society.[3] If this is not
clearly understood, then a call for widespread property
ownership and for a legal structure that supports such
distributed ownership, will be judged from presuppositions that place "an absolute value" on property
because they do not acknowledge any hierarchy of
human and divine goods. But when we do acknowledge
such a hierarchy we will recognize the inherent limits
of private ownership and see things in a different light.

2) Different types of corporate entities have different
reasons for existing and therefore different relationships
to the common good. Business corporations are less
necessary to the common good than are universities, say,
thus providing a justification for the tax-exempt status
of the latter since they are meant to fulfill important
public purposes. It is not necessary to specify here all
the implications of these varying kinds of corporate
property owners and ownership, but it is important

---

[3] For Pius XI, see his encyclical *Quadragesimo Anno*, nos. 117–19.
For John Paul II, see *Centesimus Annus*, no. 13.

to establish the principle that property, or whatever owner or kind, must be justified on the basis of its relationship to the common good.

3) What I called "private communal property," has at times assumed great importance, due in part to the state of technology. In the Middle Ages in Europe property in land was frequently held in common, which facilitated joint work such as harvesting. What is known as the "medieval open field" was a situation in which villages held land in common and allotted its use, some for individual use, some for common use, such as grazing.[4] This was not in opposition to individual or family property but simply a recognition that according to the demands of the common good, not all property need be owned or held in the same way. The point of this is not that cooperative ownership is always better, but that it sometimes is, and we should consider each case on its merits.

4) As to state property, beyond the obvious cases of state ownership of buildings and other facilities necessary for governmental functioning, we should consider these words of Pius XI in *Quadragesimo Anno*. In his discussion of socialism he notes

> that type of social authority, which, in violation of all justice has been seized and usurped by the owners of wealth. This authority in fact belongs not to the individual owners, but to the State. . . .
>
> For it is rightly contended that certain forms of property must be reserved to the State, since they carry with them an opportunity of domination too great to be left to private individuals without injury to the community at large. (no. 114)

Writers have identified as possible examples of such

---

[4] Cf. the interesting discussion of property rights focusing on common ownership, including family ownership, in Robert C. Ellickson, "Property in Land," *Yale Law Journal*, vol. 102, no. 6, April 1993, pp. 1315–1395. It includes an account of the medieval open field on pages 1388–1394.

property which is vital to the functioning of a social order as finance, utilities, transportation and certain primary industries, or perhaps the manufacture of armaments. No doubt different times and places will necessitate different arrangements in this matter, and the point is not to specify in advance what is proper, but to recognize the principle that state ownership in some cases is suggested or even required by the common good. Moreover where occupational groups or guilds are stronger and more active, state ownership is likely to be less frequently required, since these groups can take over functions which otherwise would need to be allotted to the government itself, as we saw in a previous chapter in the case of finance and the issuing of money.

Now objections to the understanding of property which I have just set forth generally rest upon an erroneous understanding of property rights, an understanding based upon the ideas of such Enlightenment philosophers as John Locke, that the right to property is absolute and that human positive law plays no part in setting limits to the right to property. The quotations from papal documents I have provided ought to be sufficient to dispel that idea for those who recognize the authority of such documents. But there is another objection that can arise, even on the part of those what might agree in theory that property has a purpose and that excessive amounts of kinds of property can violate that purpose. This objection is: Who will decide what are the reasonable limits on property? And what is to prevent restrictions on property ownership that might be reasonable at first from degenerating into tyranny?

I acknowledge the real truth that underlies this objection. Rulers and their bureaucracies, even without becoming tyrants, can become officious busybodies. And worse than that, real tyrants are not unknown to history. But such fears concern, or ought to concern, *all* human laws, not simply those designed to regulate property ownership. That is, there seems to me no reason why we need fear that a government will abuse its power over our property any more than over any other area of our life. Governments have always had many ways of abusing their power, and there are more direct ways of silencing opposition or doing away with troublemakers than by excessive tightening up of laws on property ownership.

Moreover, when we consider legal restrictions on property, we ought to have in mind, in most cases, not so much legal limits or, still less, confiscation, but rather simply measures designed to make excessive property ownership difficult and burdensome. One would hope that the occasions on which a government would have to exercise its powers of confiscation would be rare. But it is always proper to structure the laws and institutions of society such that while it is easy to acquire property sufficient for family life, it is not easy to acquire large amounts of property, especially property that carries the danger of dominating economic or political life for private ends. A society cannot legislate chastity, for example, but it can, by its laws and institutions, encourage chastity and discourage unchastity.

Note also the special case of property in land. Land, like water, is a primary good, and unlike farm animals or crops or manufactured goods, can be added to only in the rarest of circumstances, and is absolutely necessary for sustaining human life. And although the supply of land can hardly be increased, land can be rendered unusable for all practical purposes for long periods, for example, by pollution with toxic wastes. Thus there is additional justification for recognizing the interests of society above that of individual owners and treating land as a special form of property. If someone destroys a house or other building it can always be rebuilt or replaced, but if someone treats land in such a way that it becomes unusable, this is an offense against society or humanity in general. To quote Pope Leo again, "the earth, though divided among private owners, ceases not thereby to minister to the needs of all; for there is no one who does not live on what the land brings forth" (*Rerum Novarum*, no. 8). Property in land, therefore, can hardly be simply ranked with other kinds of property, and, in a special sense, is held in trust for the benefit of the common good.

The fundamental point of this discussion of property is that, like all other economic or social functions and institutions, it bears a relationship to the common good from which it draws its rights, its duties and its limits. It is not simply something that *exists*, but is part of the whole hierarchy and complex of human institutions which support humanity in this life and which, when rightly used, will assist us toward the next life. As Pius XI pointed out

> reason itself clearly deduces from the nature of things and from the individual and social character of man, what is the end and object of the whole economic order assigned by God the Creator.
>
> For it is the moral law alone which commands us to seek in all our conduct our supreme and final end, and to strive directly in our specific actions for those ends which nature, or rather, the Author of Nature, has established for them, duly subordinating the particular to the general. If this law be faithfully obeyed, the result will be that particular economic aims, whether of society as a body or of individuals, will be intimately linked with the universal teleological order, and as a consequence we shall be led by progressive stages to the final end of all, God Himself, our highest and lasting good. (*Quadragesimo Anno*, nos. 42 and 43)

10
An Embedded Economy

Probably nearly everyone would assent to the statement that the economy is meant to serve society, not the other way around. But despite the verbal acquiescence that would most likely be given to this statement, it is my contention that in fact for modernity most often the very opposite is true: society in fact serves the economy. As it has been expressed, "society itself becomes an 'adjunct' of the market." [1]

When the economy serves society it can be said to be embedded in society, that is, it is not primarily looked at as a mechanism, separate or partially separate from society with its own laws and principles, but as a subordinate part of society, whose goals it shares and supports. But when the economy is not embedded in society it functions more or less as a separate and even superior principle, and economic or financial considerations alone determine economic decisions, rather than economic considerations being seen as only part of the complex of factors which should be taken into account in any economic decision.

Consider the question of wages. Under capitalism wages are looked at pretty much only from a purely economic angle. Opinion in the United States tends to regard wages as simply an economic or financial transaction between employer and employee, which in the end comes down to: What is the marginal productivity of the worker? What does he contribute to the profitability of the enterprise? And then, what wage does

---

[1] Ellen Meiksins Wood, "From Opportunity to Imperative: The History of the Market," *Monthly Review*, vol. 46, no. 3, July–August 1994, p. 20.

his contribution justify? Seldom is the wage looked at as the means of support for a family, hence for a community, a parish, a state or region. Those factors are ignored, they are not considered as relevant to the question. But wages and jobs are more than a financial transaction between an individual and a firm, they are an important nexus in the complex of human social relationships which make up a community. Only when their place in society is recognized, and the financial considerations balanced by other concerns, can we say that an economy is embedded in, and hence, subordinate to, the needs of society.

When a company decides to move its factories to another location, where labor costs are cheaper, seldom is there any condemnation of such a move based on the integrity of the society which is being abandoned. Neighborhoods, parishes, cities, entire regions effectively die, but this is seen as something inevitable, simply the way economies work. And indeed, this is true. As long as economic activity is conducted with little or no regard for anything beyond economic considerations, people and the societies they have built will always be at the mercy of those who hold economic power, companies whose only concern is maintaining their profits, or who are even motivated by trying to increase their profit margins over against their rivals. This is not to say that economic factors can be ignored or wished away. Obviously they must be taken into account, but taken into account not exclusively, but along with other equally or more important factors.

Another example of the lack of an embedded economy can be found in the field of education. In the United States education, and especially higher education, is regarded most often as merely an economic investment. The fact that, at least till recently, those with degrees generally have fared better financially is the justification for higher education most often advanced, and advanced with seldom any objection. Now that this appears to be changing, the discussion centers around whether getting a degree still "pays," whether it is still a good investment. Education as initiation into our historical culture, as enabling one to be free of the prejudices of one's time and place, as learning to clearly think—though occasionally such considerations are brought up, perhaps in graduation addresses, for the most part the discussion of higher education is conducted solely around questions of the return on an individual's financial investment.

The same merely economic considerations dominate much of our discussion of both environmental and consumer protections. Will protecting the environment or protecting the consumer destroy jobs? How often is the question even raised as to whether having a job which at the same time subjects the worker or his family or society in general to unhealthy or unsafe conditions or products is a good thing or not? For even a job that pays well but that at the same time injures the worker's health hardly seems like a good bargain.

Now how did such a situation, a situation in which economic or financial considerations are the only factors, or the chief factors, considered, arise? I think that the following from Hilaire Belloc exposes the root of the matter.

> But wealth obtained indirectly as profit out of other men's work, or by process of exchange, becomes a thing abstracted from the process of production. As the interest of a man in things diminishes, his interest in abstract wealth—money—increases. The man who makes a table or grows a crop makes the success of the crop or the table a test of excellence. The intermediary who buys and sells the crop or the table is not concerned with the goodness of table or crop, but with the profit he makes between their purchase and sale. In a productive society the

superiority of the things produced is the measure
of success: in a Commercial society the amount of
wealth accumulated by the dealer is the measure
of success.[2]

If we ask ourselves the question of why mankind
needs economic activity, the answer is obvious. God has
created us in such a way that we need external goods
just to survive, let alone to live a truly human life. It is
thus the *things* that an economy produces, the goods and
services, that are important. But a commercial society
will always tend to change the focus from things to
money. "As the interest of a man in things diminishes,
his interest in abstract wealth — money — increases." A
craftsman obviously desires to support himself and his
family by his work — but most often he is truly interested in his craft, and sees it as something more than
simply a means of making money. He takes pride in
his skill and in his productions. A capitalist owner of a
factory, on the other hand, tends to be more interested
simply in sales. He himself does not work in the factory,
he himself does not have the pride of the craftsman. Of
course there are exceptions to this, both ways, but this
is how capitalism generally operates. In the most developed type of capitalist arrangement, the corporation,
the legal owners of the corporation, the shareholders,
often scarcely know or care what the firm actually does,
so long as their dividend checks keep coming or the
value of their stock rises. They are completely divorced
from the production process and their interest is entirely
in financial gain. Hence the money standard reigns
supreme in a capitalist or commercial society, and this
standard tends to infect all other areas of life.

God certainly ordained that mankind should engage
in economic activity — but economic activity directed

---

[2] *An Essay on the Nature of Contemporary England* (New York: Sheed
& Ward, 1937), p. 67.

toward *use,* toward "things," not "abstract wealth." The dominance of markets, and hence the distortion or perversion of what an economy was meant to be, has had profoundly negative effects on human life. It has created the commercial society, in which money and exchange have taken the place of production for use and the economy is no longer embedded in society.

> No society could, naturally, live for any length of time unless it possessed an economy of some sort; but previously to our time no economy has ever existed that, even in principle, was controlled by markets.... Though the institution of the market was fairly common since the later Stone Age, its role was no more than incidental to economic life.[3]

If we are to have an economy that is embedded in society, rather than one that subjects society to itself, then both our thinking and our institutions must change. But for our thinking to change, our understanding of what economic activity is and how it operates must first change. That is the necessary first step to establishing an economy that is both sane and just and truly serves the needs of mankind.

---

[3] Karl Polany, *The Great Transformation* (Boston: Beacon, c. 1944), p. 43.

Alternative Schools
of Economic Thought

In this book I have taken as my continual foil the neoclassical or mainstream school of economics and one of its chief spokesmen, Paul Samuelson. But there are other schools of economics, other ways to understand how economies function. The best way to make these other schools known to readers seemed to me to attach my review of the book, *Why Economists Disagree: An Introduction to the Alternative Schools of Thought*, edited by David L. Prychitko (Albany: State University of New York Press, c. 1998). The review originally appeared in *The Chesterton Review*, vol. 25, no. 3, August 1999, and has been slightly edited here.

Although both G. K. Chesterton and Hilaire Belloc devoted a significant amount of their writing to what might be called economic topics, professional economists are not likely to give much attention to their writings. This is because economics has built itself up as a science (in the modern sense of that term), complete with often arcane mathematical diagrams and equations. In fact, economics strives to be as much like physics as possible. But this description of economics in fact applies fully only to one school, the mainstream neoclassical school, which conceives of economics as a study of individuals seeking to maximize their welfare by means of a semi-automatic process with little reference to the culture or institutions within which these individuals exist. This approach to economics took its rise in the 18th century with Adam Smith and continued to develop with thinkers such as David Ricardo and John Stuart Mill. The reader will note that these are writers steeped in the classical liberalism of John Locke, a liberalism based moreover on Locke and Hume's criticisms of metaphysics as well as on their social and political thought.

Those of us who consider the Distributist tradition of economic thought to be valuable should welcome the volume under consideration here, for as its subtitle states, it is an introduction to *alternative* schools of economic thought. The book is a collection of essays, some previously published, written by economists teaching at U. S., English and Dutch universities, which present and explore these alternatives to mainstream neoclassical economics. These schools vary widely in why and how they disagree with the reigning neoclassical school. But all of them believe that mainstream economics is chiefly interested in constructing a neat theoretical model, even though this model may little resemble the real world of economic phenomena.

Another pervasive criticism of mainstream economics made in this volume is its hostility to methodological questions.

> Most economists follow George Stigler's professional advice: Don't think about methodological or philosophical issues until you retire. Mainstream economists are taught to do economics *first* and philosophize *last*, if at all. (p. 13)

But of course we cannot perform any activity without at least implicitly following some philosophical theory. So that mainstream economists *do* do philosophy — just that it is hidden from them. In one of the most interesting essays in this collection, Tony Lawson, writing from a Post-Keynesian perspective, identifies the philosophical roots of mainstream economics in the epistemology of David Hume. Hume, of course, was radically hostile to metaphysics, and Lawson's arguments make clear that it is in its very roots that neoclassical economic theory is tainted. The fact that the alternative metaphysic Lawson offers as a substitute for Hume, which he calls transcendental realism, is not very convincing philosophically does not make his criticisms any less valid.

The alternative economic school that is usually considered closest to neoclassicalism is the so-called Austrian school, so named because its founders and most notable exponents were from Austria. Readers will probably recognize the names of Frederick von Hayek and Ludwig von Mises, both of whom are associated with a libertarian economic philosophy, which Austrian theorists often incline toward. Austrian economics, however, in its most basic formulations differs from the mainstream synthesis in that it gives much more weight to factors such as time, uncertainty and competition. But it shares with neoclassical theory a deductive method and "it retains the idea of an abstract and purposeful individual" (p. 157), i.e., some version of the infamous "economic man."

Other theoretical approaches that differ more widely from mainstream economics are Post-Keynesianism and Institutionalism. The former seeks to build on the insights of John Maynard Keynes, and believes that the contemporary neoclassical synthesis has essentially trivialized Keynes and tacitly abandoned his most important theoretical positions. Institutionalism attempts to approach the study of economics from a new standpoint, and realizes that our economic choices are not made in some abstract realm, but are influenced by the milieu in which we live.

> . . . institutionalists argue that the concept of *the* market (or *the* economy) is a chimera. Market institutions are *embedded* within a panoply of social,

> cultural, and political institutions, and markets
> shape, and are shaped by, institutions. To isolate
> and analyze something called the market . . . is a
> highly, misleading scientific abstraction, and an
> ideological confusion. (p. 10)

Among the most important of these institutions is the legal system itself, for matters such as property rights, forms of corporate governance, the rights of labor to organize, taxation, etc., are all shaped or determined by the legal system. To attempt to isolate the economic system from the other systems which function alongside of it would at best yield only a partial view of reality, at worst a wholly fictitious castle in the air.

Of special interest to readers of this *Review* is the chapter by William R. Waters of DePaul University, "Social Economics: A Solidarist Perspective." Solidarism is the name given by the German Jesuit economist Heinrich Pesch to the system he formulated based on Catholic social teaching. Waters characterizes the differences between, on the one hand, the Christian and traditional view and, on the other, modern mainstream economics as follows: 1) Mainstream economics regards the economy as essentially self-regulating. Thus free competition is the logical force to rule economic activity. A solidarist economics, on the other hand, takes account of the cultural, governmental and institutional systems in which economic actors in fact live and work. People do not respond to economic choices after the manner of atoms reacting with one another, and even when they may be seeking to maximize their individual or family welfare with no thought for the common good, they nevertheless react within the cultural, legal and technological framework that characterizes their society. 2) For mainstream economics the *individual* is the "basic unit of the economy," while for solidarism it is the *person*, recalling John Paul II's rich discourse on the person as foundation of social life. 3) The mainstream economic model, in order to approximate as much as possible the hard sciences, concentrates on the certainty of our knowledge of future economic events, while

> Solidarism does not accept this principle of certainty, so to the solidarists economics is not a natural science. Economics does not attain "scientific status" because free decision-making is not compatible with the rationalistic assumption of certainty. Economics is a softer discipline — a moral science. (p. 184)

4) Finally, neoclassical economics regards *contracts* as the hallmark of social and economic life. Contracts are free agreements made by presumably rational economic actors, by "economic men." But solidarism looks instead at *status*, that is, at what human persons are prior to any contracts they may enter into. An example of these contrasting methods is Leo XIII's statement that despite what agreements (contracts) may be made with regard to wages between employers and employees,

> there is a dictate of nature more imperious and more ancient than any bargain between man and man, that the remuneration must be enough to support the wage-earner in reasonable and frugal comfort. If through necessity or fear of a worse evil, the workman accepts harder conditions because an employer or contractor will give him no better, he is the victim of force and injustice. (*Rerum Novarum*, no. 45)

Leo XIII clearly recognizes that status (the nature of man) is prior to contract, but in addition he recognizes that it is vain to abstract contractual behavior from the actual historical context in which it takes place ("If through necessity or fear of a worse evil, the workman accepts harder conditions…. "). Any discussion of the morality of wages that pretends that there is always equality in bargaining power between employer and employee is not a discussion that has to do with the world in which we actually live.

Waters places his solidarism within the tradition and thought of Christian Europe:

> The dispute is about method, and is between those who accept an Aristotelian outlook on the nature of economic studies and those who have adopted the "modern" Enlightenment approach. The Aristotelian view . . . identifies the study of economic life as focused on satisfying the material needs of the community to permit it to survive and reproduce itself. This view dominated Europe during the Middle Ages but fell out of favor almost completely with the rise of the social philosophy of the Enlightenment and its legitimate offspring, classical economics. The latter focuses upon the decision-making behavior of the individual and the maximization of individual and collective welfare. (p. 202)

In other words, (neo)classical economics fails even to inquire if economic activity has a final cause, that is, it does not ask *why* it is that man engages in activities of production and exchange. It examines it after a positivist manner, merely as an isolated phenomenon, with its own laws, and assumes that the motives of the individual economic actor are all that exist. But a Christian thinker who really bases his views on Christian philosophy and theology, will realize that all human activity is connected. Neither economic behavior nor economic science can be autonomous, but must be related to moral theology, to the philosophy of man and to political philosophy.

Waters also discusses a few firms which have attempted to operate according to solidarist principles, or who have been forced to do so in order to overcome worker disaffection and prevent a business from closing. The example that he admires most is the Mondragon cooperatives in the Basque country of Spain, started in the 1950s by Fr. José María Arizmendi. Mondragon has definitely been an economic success. Its finance arm, Caja Laboral Popular, exists to help and guide new ventures. Yet its "resources are applied to the social goals of community and regional development with locally based small and medium sized businesses." Despite this, or perhaps because of it, it has done very well. "Its record of starting more than a hundred firms, including some of the largest manufacturers in Spain, with only three failures . . . is remarkable when contrasted with the high business failure rate in America" (p. 201).

After Waters' essay on social economics, the next three essays in the book deal with Marxist economic theories. In view of the collapse of the Soviet Union and most other communist states, many Marxists today are at pains to distinguish their positions from the discredited "official Marxism" that prevailed in the Soviet bloc. Although as Pius XI made clear in *Quadragesimo Anno*, because of their philosophical foundations, no form of Marxism or socialism is ever acceptable to Catholic thinkers, it does not follow from this that we can never learn anything from them. Indeed, in a passage from the same encyclical, Pius says that the economic proposals of the more moderate socialists of his day "often strikingly approach the just demands of Christian social reformers" (*Quadragesimo Anno*, no. 113). So, then, in the discussion of various Marxist and kindred theories in this volume, we may well discover some truths.

In the first of these essays, "Comparison of Marxism and Institutionalism," there is much to interest a Distributist. The essay is organized around a series of questions which are posited first to an Institutionalist, then to a Marxist. Perhaps the most interesting of the questions is, "Can the social sciences be ahistorical?" Mainstream economics is a deductive science, and just as physics does not inquire whether the objects which it deals with exist in China or in Chile, in the fifth century or the twenty-first, so mainstream economists tend to do likewise. But in the nineteenth century certain German economists, known as the German Historical School, insisted otherwise, namely that the same economic solution or principle might bring about very different results depending on the circumstances in which it is applied. The example instanced is relevant to policy debates today.

> One obvious example of the need for historical specificity is the analysis of the free trade doctrine. As the German scholars realized full well, free trade was great for the British in 1870 since British industries were firmly established by then and since British interests were protected by the British navy. But free trade was disadvantageous for the Germans in 1870 since their infant industries faced imports from mature British producers at home and faced British interests backed up by the British navy abroad. (p. 217)

But this truth, that economics cannot prescind from historical circumstances, goes deeper and challenges the entire concept of the "economic man," that wonderful creature who spends his life continually buying cheap and selling dear. In chapter two of his classic work, *The Protestant Ethic and the Spirit of Capitalism*, Max Weber recounts the modus operandi of European cloth merchants before they became infected with the spirit of capitalism.

> The number of business hours was very moderate, perhaps five to six a day, sometimes considerably less; in the rush season, where there was one, more. Earnings were moderate; enough to lead a respectable life and in good times to put away a little. On the whole, relations among competitors were relatively good, with a large degree of agreement on the fundamentals of business. A long daily visit to the

tavern, with often plenty to drink, and a congenial circle of friends, made life comfortable and leisurely.

The point here is that because of their cultural milieu these merchants were satisfied with a moderate and customary income. They did not seek to maximize their acquisition of money. It is simply not true that everywhere and always men seek the highest returns and drive the hardest bargains they can. In fact, unless and until a capitalist culture tells them to do so, they will usually be content with a traditional standard of living.

The happy situation described above, Weber continues, broke down when some new merchant who believed in working long hours and getting a maximum return from his work, introduced new methods which everyone else was forced to adopt if he did not want to go out of business. "The old leisurely and comfortable attitude toward life gave way to a hard frugality...."

A similar point about even more contemporary economic actors is made in the second of these three essays, "Postmodernism, Marxism, and the Critique of Modern Economic Thought."

> Consider, for example, the "normal" activity of consumers. They often shop in the same locations, purchasing many of the same goods, even when prices vary (sometimes considerably) from one marketplace to another and new products are placed on the shelves.... Similarly, firms often negotiate long-term contracts with other firms ... precisely in order to "stabilize" deliveries and to avoid the "disorder" attendant upon the continual recontracting and renegotiating that would be necessary every time the price or quality of a commodity changes. In neither case — and these may be the norm rather than the exception — do markets exhibit the disorder... implicit in those neoclassical stories that portray the instantaneous reactions of consumers and producers through the metaphors of supply and demand.... (p. 252)

The last of the three essays dealing with Marxism, "Toward a Socialism of the Future, in the Wake of the Demise of the Socialism of the Past," is the most interesting to a Distributist. It seeks to distance itself from the "official Marxism" of the Communist bloc by advocating variant kinds of socialism, discussing both "market socialism" and "participatory socialism." In an introductory section the author suggests a four point summary of the goals of *any* socialism, and we should note goal number 3, which reminds us of Pius XI's judgment which I quoted above, that socialist aims can "often strikingly approach the just demands of Christian social reformers." Goal number three is thus:

> 3. *Solidarity*: as against the celebration of the individual under capitalism, socialism calls for the promotion of solidarity among members of communities extending from the neighborhood to the whole of society—encouraging people to develop the sense and the reality of themselves as social rather than simply individual beings. (p. 275)

There is nothing a Catholic or a Distributist could object to here, except to point out that socialism provides absolutely no foundation for such solidarity. For in view of the Fall, human nature is now so weak that a bond merely earthly will not stand for long against the passions and selfishness that too often flow from the human heart.

Nevertheless we can look at this discussion of market socialism and participatory socialism and see parallels to Distributist and Catholic social thought. Let us begin with market socialism. Market socialism has its roots in the 1920s as an alternative to the Bolshevik regime that was then consolidating its power in Russia. As the name implies, it desired to retain the institution of the market, though heavily regulated by the government, but toward the question of ownership it assumed a more socialistic stance. That is, some market socialists advocated the ownership of all productive property by the state (or the workers in the enterprise), although others allowed for private ownership of small businesses and reserved to the state only "the major sectors and/ or the most important enterprises in the economy . . . " (p. 280). It is these latter thinkers that I find most interesting, for did not Pius XI say:

> For it is rightly contended that certain forms of property must be reserved to the State, since they carry with them an opportunity of domination too great to be left to private individuals without injury to the community at large.
>
> Just demands and desires of this kind contain nothing opposed to Christian truth, nor are they in any sense peculiar to socialism. Those therefore who look for nothing else, have no reason for becoming socialists. (*Quadragesimo Anno*, nos. 114–115)

It is often forgotten that, while remaining always implacable to the spirit or philosophical basis of socialism, there is sometimes a remarkable convergence between the specific economic proposals of Catholic social teaching and those of some of the moderate forms of socialism. Nor should we forget the similar words of that arch-distributist, Hilaire Belloc. In the following passage Belloc is speaking of enterprises that cannot easily be broken up into smaller units.

> State ownership is better, of course, than ownership by a few very rich individuals, or even than ownership by many small shareholders who are at the mercy of a few rich ones, as they are under our English company law. . . . A chartered guild composed of the workers in the system would be one form of communal system securing a better distribution of wealth. . . . (*The Restoration of Property*, chap. 4)

Belloc's ideal, and mine too, is for property to be divided as much as possible. It is strange that even the moderate socialists writing here do not discuss this, but are concerned instead only with the management of large units, and if they allow for private ownership of small business it is almost as an afterthought to which they devote little attention. It is understandable that men brought up in this civilization will tend to think only in terms of the large, but surely our *ideal* can be for well distributed productive property, a position, moreover, that the Supreme Pontiffs have advocated since at least Leo XIII.

Going from market socialism to participatory socialism is like going from the 1930s to the 1960s, for the latter system is reminiscent of the participatory democracy of that decade. Not wanting any form of the market, its device for allocating economic resources will be by participatory and decentralized discussion, or, as the author suggests, by an endless and ultimately impractical series of meetings.

The basic decision-making units of the participatory system are typically workplace workers' councils and neighborhood consumers' councils, in which production and consumption decisions are made collectively by workplace and neighborhood communities, respectively. But these basic decision-making units are embedded in a larger network of related politically constituted bodies, designed to bring to bear relevant considerations and concerns that transcend the scope of individual workplaces and neighborhoods. A critical role in the network of non-market decision-making institutions is played by various planning boards, which are responsible for collecting and dispensing information and for coordinating the decisions of separate councils and entities in such a way that decentralized production and consumption plans emanating from all the workplaces and neighborhoods ultimately converge to a feasible overall pattern of production and consumption. (p. 288)

It is no wonder that the author says,

> The mere listing of these requirements is enough to generate skepticism about whether and how they can possibly be met [and] . . . even if all the needed information could be accurately compiled, wouldn't participatory planning require each individual to dedicate so much time, interest and energy to assessing the information and participating in decision-making meetings that most people would get sick and tired of doing it? (p. 290)

Of course, all this apparatus of participatory socialism is for the laudable goal of avoiding the central bureaucracies that characterized the Soviet bloc. But for most of us, there are better ways of avoiding bureaucracies and better ways of spending our time.

Following these chapters on socialism we come to rather different ground. First is the essay, "The Feminist Challenge to Neoclassical Economics." Though there are varieties of feminist economics, just as there are varieties of feminism, all of them in one way or another share in the fundamental errors that afflict feminism: an unwillingness to recognize that there are natural differences between men and women and that these natural differences necessarily have social and economic consequences (although this does not mean that all the changes in the political or social status of women in the twentieth century were necessarily wrong), and a belief that since our tradition of religious, philosophical and political thought was created largely by males, it necessarily is unfair, exclusionary or oppressive toward females.

Mainstream economics, in a kind of exception to its preoccupation with the lone individual, did not attempt to use its analytic technique to examine relations *within* the family, but treated the family as a unit. And this was all for the good, as far as it went, for it was a kind of tacit acknowledgment that not all human relations should be brought within the cash nexus. But the aims of feminist economists, at least as portrayed in this essay, definitely include examining relations within families, sometimes to the point of absurdity. "Sen concludes that there is inequality in the distribution of food within the family. Evidence from rural Bangladesh and West Bengal suggests that women generally receive less calories than men . . . " (p. 311). But at the same time, part of their agenda is "to conduct research free from androcentric bias" (p. 310). Yet it would seem to me that the desire to bring everything under the cool analytic technique of economics, to use quantitative tools to enter the family, is simply to *extend* what are often seem as specifically androcentric prejudices, the supposed hyperrationalism of the male. It may be, however, that to these feminist economists, "research free from androcentric bias" simply means that women want to be like males, equating equality with sameness. The preoccupation in this chapter with income equality in the family would tend to support this interpretation. In any case, feminist economists, like all feminists, need to come to terms with the fact of natural differences between the sexes. Whatever social arrangements we may deem best, any that fail to take account of these natural differences are founded on myth.

The final three chapters deal with issues of economic methodology or philosophy, and all of them illustrate the difficulty that thinkers have in coping with philosophical questions when they lack an adequate philosophical structure and background. Like sociology and political science, economics has ambitions to be the architectonic science, using its methods to explain everything, or at least everything pertaining to mankind. Thus one can find economics articles dealing with education, marriage, employment discrimination, etc. Yet economics, which began as a subdivision of philosophy, broke away and picked up in the process

a very questionable (but largely unrecognized) philosophical framework, can never fulfill such a role. Even
aside from its erroneous philosophical presuppositions,
it is necessarily limited in its scope or formal object.
In the first of these three methodological essays one
sees the considerable confusion into which the author
frequently falls, even though he is aware of the shortcomings of economics, of "the incredible complexity
of human nature which was disregarded by traditional
[economic] theory..." (p. 342). Having set up a kind of
straw man, or a man stripped of most of his real human
characteristics, some economists then find that their
homo economicus does not fit the real world. The better
ones are aware of this and cast about for some way out,
while those content to continue in the mainstream
either ignore the problem or persuade themselves that
it doesn't matter.

The next essay is even more critical of economics, for
the author boldly proclaims that all economic models
and the policy prescriptions that flow from them are
"tautological (circular)... the conclusions and implications are not independent but are derived from the
assumptions...; choice of assumptions constitutes
choice of conclusions and implications" (p. 347). In the
face of this the author laudably recommends modesty
and restraint on the part of economists, with a "less
pretentious status and less demanding desires, perhaps... on a par, as Keynes said, with dentists" (p. 362).

The last essay is a dialogue between two economists,
one a neoclassical and the other an institutionalist or
Marxist. Both are critical of what they regard as the
pretensions of modernism, without however, embrac-
ing postmodernism, and both think that the neoclassical approach to economics has too often ignored the
reality of the world of actual economic actors: "our
students... are trained to think that economics is a
matter of engineering math" (p. 379). Again one can

see economists struggling to get away from clearly inadequate theories, but without a clear idea of where to go or from where to get help. These essays indicate again the truth that there is no substitute for philosophy, and that to approach philosophical issues with a methodology derived from other branches of knowledge will guarantee a failure.

The book ends with a bibliographic essay by the editor, a very helpful discussion of further reading concerning all of the economic schools and issues presented here. Since each chapter also includes a bibliography supplied by its author(s), there is a wealth of suggestions for further study. Although the titles listed for solidarism need to be supplemented with the papal social encyclicals and their considerable commentaries, and with economic works in the Distributist tradition, still they are a useful starting point.

Some of the chapters in the first part of this book, notably Alfred Eichner's and J. A. Kregel's "An Essay on Post-Keynesian Theory: A New Paradigm in Economics," are nearly impossible for one not conversant with econometrics, for it includes a number of the diagrams and equations which adorn, or perhaps disfigure, most economic writing. But in the second part of the book, most of the essays are accessible for one with some acquaintance with and interest in the subject. And, moreover, this is a subject that ought to be of interest to any educated Catholic or Chestertonian. For it is not something only of interest to narrow specialists, the "dismal science" of Carlyle, nor is it only part of the partisan world of politicians and pundits. The arrangements that a society makes for its economic activity have profound moral and cultural consequences, consequences too important to be left to those trained in the narrow discipline of neoclassical economics. Thus, because economics is too important to be left to the economists, it must become the concern of the theologian, of the moral and political philosopher, of the citizen. Though this volume is not an all-sufficient vade mecum, it is a helpful introduction to some of the moral, social and philosophical issues that economics raises. Therefore I recommend it both to readers interested in economics — and to those who ought to become so.

APPENDIX II

The Butcher, the Baker, the Candlestick Maker

Much of this book has been about our economic institutions and about the need to make important changes in them. And this is important, for to imagine that we can rely solely on moral exhortation to bring about economic justice is sadly mistaken. But while a change in laws and institutions is necessary, at the same time such changes will accomplish little or nothing if there is not at the same time an effort to change our thinking, to instill a new spirit into our economic life. In this chapter, beginning with a quotation from Adam Smith, we will examine our attitudes toward economic conduct, and see how such a new spirit is necessary if we are ever to establish an economy that approximates to the norms of justice.

There is a well-known passage in Adam Smith's *Wealth of Nations* (book I, chapter 2) that runs thus:

> It is not from the benevolence of the butcher, the brewer, or the baker that we expect our dinner, but from their regard to their own interest. We address ourselves, not to their humanity but to their self-love, and never talk to them of our own necessities but of their advantages.

Although Adam Smith sometimes displays more knowledge both of human nature and of how an economy actually operates than do today's supporters of a free market, nevertheless it would appear that this passage can reasonably be regarded as nothing more than a simple affirmation of basic self-interest, self-interest which is held to be the proper and only effective motive for economic activity. But let us look at this statement both in light of its application to the individual tradesman or craftsman — the butcher, the brewer, the baker — and as applied to the economy and society as a whole.

When we look at the individual craftsman or merchant about whose motives Adam Smith's speaks with such confidence, we might raise two questions. The first concerns the "self-love" and "advantages" which are alleged to be the sole motive of these tradesmen. For self-love, or self-interest, is susceptible of two meanings. By the first is meant an ordered and proper regard for oneself, a regard compatible indeed with love of neighbor and even sanctity. But by the second is meant a self-interest which is disordered in that it has no care for the needs of others and seeks its own desires exclusively. If it happens also to benefit another, this is neither here nor there. This second type is one of the effects of the sin of our first parents, one of the results of original sin. Since Smith contrasts self-interest with both "benevolence" and "humanity" it is reasonable to think that he is speaking of the second, of the disordered kind of self-love.

Supporters of the kind of economics that stems from the tradition of Adam Smith generally take as one of their fundamental points that this second type of self-interest is wonderfully fitted to supply the needs of society. The butcher wants money, we want meat, the exchange is perfect. Christian supporters of this type of economics might assert that they do not necessarily praise the butcher's motives, but that, since they exist and are so ubiquitous, we must acknowledge and make use of them. Otherwise we will attempt to conduct our economy on false principles and end up having to use the heavy and inefficient hand of the state to motivate producers and sellers.

But how curious is this idea! It is certainly odd that Christian defenders of self-interest are quite comfortable with accepting behavior based on man's sinful tendencies as the foundation for the economy, something they would probably denounce in any other area of social life. For example, if one were to argue that the abolition of marriage and the free mixing of the sexes was the best way to propagate the human race, since this is based on people's natural and ineradicable inclinations, this would hardly be acceptable to them, but with scarcely a demur they allow, and often indeed praise, behavior founded on human greed as the best way to run an economy, and this despite the fact that Sacred Scripture and the entire tradition of the Church condemn the motive of greed at least as strongly as the motive of lust.

Secondly, if we look more closely at Smith's assertion, is he in fact correct in thinking that the butcher or brewer is motivated solely by self-regard of the second sort discussed above? It is true that we expect a natural desire on the part of a butcher or a brewer to make a living by his trade, but this natural and proper concern for his own welfare does not necessarily mean that he is motivated solely by a disordered self-interest. Every physician expects to make a living by the practice of medicine, but the expectation is that he is as much interested in the welfare of his patients as he is in earning his fees. There is clearly nothing wrong in someone hoping to gain a living for himself and his family by means of his work. Indeed, such an expectation is natural and laudable. But it must be carefully distinguished from behavior based solely upon greed. Most of the time people's motives will be mixed. Quite often this is not something to cause concern. But what Adam Smith does is to assume that the probably mixed motives of a tradesman, mixed between pure desire for gain, a desire to support his family, a love of his craft, and a desire to serve the public, can be reduced simply to one motive, the pure desire for gain. Not only is this usually false, but by proclaiming that we appeal not to "their humanity but to their self-love," he helps create a situation in which more and more tradesmen will begin to think of themselves, not as entrusted with meeting a public need, but as simply out to make as much for themselves as possible.

There is no essential difference between the provision of health to the community and the provision of meat or beer or bread. In each case the provider offers something necessary for human life and expects to earn a living by what he does. But the cultural expectation is that the physician is motivated by more than mere gain while the butcher and those of like trades are motivated solely or mostly by gain. As I suggested above, this cultural expectation plays some part in creating or fixing motives in the minds of individual economic actors. If a physician feels some shame because his motive is merely gain, in some cases at least he will work to better his motives by trying to incite himself to service to the community as well. But for the butcher, on the other hand, if he is continually told that self-interest is all that society has a right to expect from him, whatever nobler motives he originally had will tend to become buried under a single-minded pursuit of gain. The English economic historian Richard Tawney sums this up very well in the following passage from his book, *The Acquisitive Society*.

> The idea that there is some mysterious difference between making munitions of war and firing them, between building schools and teaching in them when built, between providing food and providing health, which makes it at once inevitable and laudable that the former should be carried on with a single eye to pecuniary gain, while the latter are conducted by professional men who expect to be paid for service but who neither watch for windfalls nor raise their fees merely because there are more sick to be cured, more children to be taught, or more enemies to be

resisted, is an illusion only less astonishing than that
the leaders of industry should welcome the insult
as an honor and wear their humiliation as a kind of
halo. The work of making boots or building a house
is in itself no more degrading than that of curing
the sick or teaching the ignorant. It is as necessary
and therefore as honorable.... It should be at least
equally free from the vulgar subordination of moral
standards to financial interests.[1]

I realize that a common objection to this is that it is
unrealistic, that even if it works to some extent in the
case of highly-educated physicians, it surely cannot
be expected to work in the case of every Tom, Dick
or Harry. But while I do not deny that sin and sordid
motives will always be present in human society, do
we expect people who are told that there are no moral
standards which apply to them to behave better than
those who are instructed as to their rights and their
corresponding duties? Conservatives (in the American
sense), who generally champion free-market economics based on self-interest, are usually quite vocal in
stressing the need and utility of high moral principles
in other areas of life, but when it comes to economics,
they seem to regard behavior based solely or mostly
upon greed as all that can be expected.

I might note that, at least by Christians, greed is
considered as a deadly sin, and that to inculcate the
doctrine that one need think only of one's own needs
and desires in his economic activity is to warp and pervert the souls of those who imbibe such ideas, deprive
them of the opportunity to develop virtues, and possibly put them on the road to Hell. I find it hard to
think that any economy which points any number of
its participants on the way to eternal punishment is
a healthy economy, regardless of how much stuff it
boasts that it can produce.

---

[1] (New York: Harcourt, Brace & World, 1920), p. 96.

Now let us turn our attention from the individual producer, his possible motives and the possible fate of his soul, to look at some of the social effects that follow from Adam Smith's dictum about the motives of tradesmen.

If we take Adam Smith at his word, that butchers have only in mind their own interest, their own self-love, their own advantages, then why, one might ask, do we expect the public's need for meat or beer or bread to be well supplied by them? If they really are utterly self-interested, will they not continually seek means by which they may supply the public with inferior products and shoddy goods? Now the defenders of an economy based upon self-interest will reply that this is impossible, at least in the long run, because if producers and sellers attempt this, then the public will eventually find this out and no longer buy from them and others instead will step into their places and make and sell quality goods. This theory works well on paper, and perhaps can be elegantly expressed by means of a graph, but it has little foundation in reality. If it were the case, would we not trust every used car dealer to give us a fair appraisal of the condition of a car, would not sellers of securities never misrepresent the condition of the firm whose securities they offer for sale, would not consumer fraud be as rare as snow in July? It is no accident that *caveat emptor*, let the buyer beware, is an oft repeated slogan in the U. S. For if a seller really has only his self-interest at heart, then he will cheat his customers whenever he thinks he can get away with it. That he can convince someone to buy a product is his sole concern. The seller gains by selling his product. If he calculates that the fraud will not be detected or that he will be able to successfully escape responsibility for it, then (on Adam Smith's view) there is nothing to deter him from cheating people as much as he can.

The incidence of consumer fraud and of shoddy products will vary considerably depending on many factors. That they are not more common is in part a tribute to the fact that, even within the culture of competitive capitalism, many people do rise above Smith's account of a craftsman and his motivations. But it is also a tribute to government laws enacted against fraud, against selling tainted food, and so on. The fact that industries try and sometimes succeed in capturing the regulatory process and controlling the agency that is supposed to regulate them is not an argument against regulation. Rather it points up the fact that until a new ethos and a different kind of regulatory process are created, capitalism will always exhibit selfish competitive strife as well as increasing efforts to make use of governmental power on behalf of private interests.

Another objection that is raised to what I say here by those who assume that only self-interested conduct can be expected from the generality of mankind, is that although free-market capitalism is not perfect, it is foolish to try to build an economy on the idea of service, since that will necessarily result in a vast increase of state power to supervise people's conduct. Instead of the effective, if imperfect, device of making use of people's natural inclinations, we will need an army of bureaucrats and inspectors to micromanage and scrutinize every aspect of the economy and of business behavior. And so, if we just allow self-interest to operate as the mainspring of economic activity, we bring about the best situation there could be, with as plentiful a supply of quality goods as we could hope to obtain.

It is certainly true that no system is perfect and that since the Fall of our first parents every institution of mankind is flawed. All we can do is to try to create the best designed institutions that we reasonably can, and try to inculcate virtue in those who are part of them. Therefore, is an economy based mostly or solely on self-interest the best we can hope for? Such an economy, I grant, is better than a pure command economy, one in which officials of the central government determine all important economic decisions. But we are not faced with only these two extremes. There are many ways we can organize an economy. Distributism, for one, offers an alternative to socialism and to self-interested free-market economics as well. Under distributism regulation and supervision of the economy, a necessity for the fallen children of Adam, would for the most part be carried out not by government officials but by the guilds (occupational groups) which are an important feature of distributism. This does not mean a command economy, rather a decentralized economy in which production is adjusted to the reasonable needs of mankind, rather than to whatever a producer can convince people to buy by means of advertising.

Ultimately the butcher, the baker and the candlestick maker will die, and when they do, they will be judged neither on how much money they have made nor on how much they have sold, but whether they have honestly worked at their trade, have offered the public quality goods and have looked upon those with whom they dealt as their brothers. If we think that our economic activity necessarily conflicts with such goals, then we need to reexamine our understanding of the economy. For here on earth we have no lasting city, and even less no lasting trade or craft or profession, and if by exercising our trade or craft we render ourselves unworthy of eternal life, we have done no favor to ourselves, to the public, or to anyone at all.

XIII BOOKS is dedicated to publishing new and vintage works centered around politics, the economy, and the family. Named after Pope Leo XIII—the pope of the "working man," whose pontificate was the first to comprehensively engage in the Church's relationship with the modern world—our imprint was born out of the conviction that we cannot separate the Catholic faith from our involvement with the world around us, and that the social doctrine of the Church, whether explicitly or implicitly, requires a commitment by Catholics to transform every aspect of the social order in conformity to the will of God. We aspire to earn a reputation amongst our readers as a reliable provider of the best the social tradition has to offer, which is rooted in our allegiance to Christ the King and passion for sharing with others the teachings of the Church.